EXPERIENCING LOURDES

EXPERIENCING LOURDES

An Intimate View of the
Miraculous Shrine and Its Pilgrims

Stephen Grosso

CHARIS
Servant Publications
Ann Arbor, Michigan

Charis Books is an imprint of Servant Publications especially designed to serve Roman Catholics.

Although the stories in this book are true, names have been changed to protect the privacy of the individuals involved.

Published by Servant Publications
P.O. Box 8617
Ann Arbor, Michigan 48107

Cover design: Diane Bareis
Cover photo: Victor Engelbert

96 97 98 99 00 10 9 8 7 6 5 4 3 2 1

Printed in the United States of America
ISBN 0-89283-962-7

LIBRARY OF CONGRESS CATALOGING-IN-PUBLICATION DATA

Grosso, Stephen
Experiencing Lourdes : an intimate view of the miraculous shrine and its pilgrims / Stephen Grosso.
    p. cm.
"Charis."
Includes bibliographical references.
ISBN 0-89283-962-7
1. Christian pilgrims and pilgrimages—France—Lourdes.   2. Spiritual biography.   3. Grosso, Stephen, 1939-   .   4. Lourdes (France)—Religious life and customs.   5. Christian shrines—France—Lourdes.   6. Lourdes (France)—Church history.   7. Mary, Blessed Virgin, Saint—Apparitions and miracles—France—Lourdes. I. Title.
BT653.G74   1996
232.91'7'094478—dc20   96-24409
                                                             CIP

CONTENTS

For my wife LaRae–
with love.

Introduction ⚜

I DID NOT DREAM that I would ever come to a place like Lourdes. Nothing in my past suggested that I would ever be pushing sick people in wheelchairs, nor that I would be intensely grateful to God for the chance to do it. Nor did I think I would ever look forward to participating in various ceremonies in the Sanctuary of Our Lady. Nor was I prepared for the subtle power of some of the visiting pilgrims I met at Lourdes who touched and affected me in such ways that I will always be grateful to them.

How it happened that I went to Lourdes to work as a *brancardier* (stretcher-bearing volunteer) began on a New York City street years ago. I was coming home from work one twilight evening. Something lying on the sidewalk caught my eye, glittering under the city streetlight. Thinking it was a coin, I picked it up. It was a gold-colored, heart-shaped, rather battered religious medal. On it was an image of the Grotto, with Bernadette kneeling before the Apparition of Our Lady.

In those days I wasn't a believer, but I put the medal in my pocket and continued on my way home. Why did I keep the medal? I was born a Roman Catholic, but had left the Church and had no defined religious belief. I had heard of Lourdes, but then everyone has heard of Lourdes. I knew Bernadette's story because I had seen the movie. I had liked the movie, though if I had been asked why I liked it I wouldn't have known what to say. After all, the story is about a fourteen-year-old girl seeing things nobody else saw. Because of this she is criticized by everybody, including her mother. She is laughed at, ridiculed, accused of playacting, harassed by the police, threatened with arrest by the municipal authorities; she is called vile names by smart alec

Parisian journalists, she endures opposition even from the local pastor of her Church, at least in the beginning.

Why did I keep medal? I kept the medal because the story of Bernadette and this mysterious Lady from another world intrigued me; because the story had in it something of what I secretly hoped existed: a world a little kinder than this one. But my hope was rooted solely in my imagination. At the time I did not see that there was anything in life beyond what one saw with the naked eye. And, like Doubting Thomas, I was not prepared to believe in anything I could not see or touch.

Since those days I have come to believe that, for many of us, disbelief in God is not voluntary. We do not choose not to believe. Rather, we stay in our disbelief for lack of knowing what to believe and how to believe; our disbelief is really a suspension of belief until in crisis the hidden God forces us to confront him.

The Lourdes medal I found on that dark street long ago was God calling me to "now," that is, the "now" of God's love that dwells in the heart of every one of us. In time I responded to God's call, and I did return to the Catholic Church. I had to pass, however, through my own trials and phases of the spirit before I was ready to go to Lourdes.

What made me go? I think the desire to visit Lourdes was born in my heart long before I thought of serving as a volunteer. I felt the Blessed Mother had been watching over me, protecting me all those years that I had lived without God. I also took the finding of the Lourdes religious medal as a sign. Again I felt she wanted me to go there. I had read everything I could on Lourdes, and learned about the Society de Notre Dame de Lourdes, a volunteer service established in 1885. I decided to join it. The volunteer service (a canonically erected confraternity since 1928) functions throughout the pilgrimage season (from Easter until October). On acceptance into the society, members volunteer to work without pay for a definite period each year.

Their duties include attending the sick, both in hospitals and at the baths, and during transport.

Going to Lourdes to serve the sick and handicapped was my way of saying "thank you" to the Blessed Mother for giving me, through her Son Jesus, the gift of faith. As it turned out, going to Lourdes to serve the sick and the handicapped only deepened the gift of faith I had received. It also brought me into contact with people of towering faith.

And this is what my book is about: People who believe in God, who love God, who remain faithful to God, even as their sickness is not taken away.

In John 20:29, we hear Jesus say, "How happy are those who believe without seeing me!" Faith, if I understand what Jesus is saying, comes from being touched by God from within one's heart. But sometimes faith is awakened through signs and wonders. Indeed, miracles and works of mercy constituted one third of Jesus' ministry on earth, and remain a potent sign of God's love for us. However, we have to face the fact that most of us who suffer with a handicap or disease or terminal illness are not miraculously cured. We may never encounter angels, nor die and come back to tell about it. Most of us are forced to take the hard route in matters of faith.

People have asked me: If most pilgrims are not cured of their infirmities, why do they return to Lourdes? For one thing, the trip to Lourdes, especially for the sick, is no joy ride. I have seen the poor come at great personal sacrifice. I have looked at the second-hand, poorly ventilated cars in which the sick are transported. One can imagine them jarred and tossed about in these cars. There are always emergencies arising; stretcher patients are helplessly dependent for their bodily needs; some are unable even to move without help.

Several times each day the train comes rattling across the French countryside into the mountain town of Lourdes.

Grinding to a stop at the train terminal, the doors of the ambulance cars open: the smell of urine, pus, and clotted blood is overpowering. These sick pilgrims have passed through an ordeal.

Not only Europeans, but Africans, Asians, Australians, North Americans, Latin Americans—badly crippled, seriously diseased people of all ages and cultures—make the same difficult trip, endure the same hardship and inconvenience.

At the train terminal, I watched as the sick passed through many hands. They are pushed through crowds, carried from train to hospice to Rosary Square to Church. They are gaped at and ogled and pitied by scores of stranger visitors.

Why do these sick pilgrims return to Lourdes, year after year, when the cure they seek does not take place? What is it that draws them? What draws them, I believe, is something that no medical man has power to give, and it is this: intimacy with God. That is, a moment of the joy of heavenly life—the life that, on faith, we believe awaits us on the other side of death. This God-life intimacy touches the soul, uplifting it, sometimes intoxicating it. Again and again I saw this divine intoxication reflected in the shining faces of sick pilgrims. I saw joy light up faces one would never dream had any reason to be joyful. My story of Gianni (see page 49), one of the most pitifully crippled pilgrims that I have ever seen, is a good example of the "spiritual miracle." Lourdes is rich with such miracles.

And what are the fruits of this God-intimacy? The fruits are this: one buries one's despair; one perseveres in one's faith; one learns patience and the hard lesson of acceptance; one endures one's suffering even though one may not understand it; above all, one is inspired to love one's neighbor. This is a paradox of the sick; often it is the sick, not the well, who love with the love of God. Indeed, I bear witness that it was the sick, sometimes terminally sick, who, often in the briefest encounter, saw me with eyes of love, who understood me as no one else did.

The sick are not always seated in wheelchairs, hobbling on crutches, or carried on stretchers; the sick not infrequently are pilgrims suffering from drug addiction, from inoperable diseases, from AIDS/HIV; the sick are pilgrims agonized by lack of faith, pilgrims seeking a meaning to life, pilgrims tortured by a wayward son or daughter. Every kind of human frailty shows up in Lourdes: the love of God turns no one away.

The problems and petitions to the Blessed Mother are endless. "Ask, and you will receive," said Jesus (Mt 7:7). And all receive: None are denied that moment of uplifting intimacy, which says, "I love you, I care about you. Trust me."

This, I believe, is the lure and power of Lourdes: that if one is not granted a miraculous cure, one is granted a miracle of the heart, one is granted a look into the life of God, and it is unforgettable. It is therefore no wonder that sick pilgrims brave every inconvenience and hardship in order to return to Lourdes.

In short, what one receives at Lourdes, regardless of one's plight or circumstance—whether sick in body or soul, whether believer or atheist—is a very special encounter with Christ the Lord through the gentle, guiding spirit of Our Lady. The only requirement is that one be open to it.

During my stay at Lourdes I kept a journal and set down accounts of the people I met there. These people moved and inspired me, first to emulate them, then to write about them. As you read, may you, too, be moved by the compassionate spirit of Our Lady of Lourdes.

CHAPTER ONE

Monsieur Eduoard

June 24. The train rattled into the station at about 5 o'clock in the afternoon. The nine-hour ride, from the Austerlitz Railroad terminal in Paris all the way down through the south of France, was ended. I looked out the window of the car and saw painted on the back of a building in huge red letters: LOURDES. A few minutes later I was walking along Rue de la Grotte, a long narrow street with rows of shops on either side. The shops sold trinkets, statuettes of the Virgin Mary, and religious bric-a-brac of every description.

Holding a suitcase in either hand, I passed through crowds of pilgrims. As I walked, it seemed as though I was being accompanied by the sound of voices that, strange to say, I felt as though I had heard before. Closing my eyes, I could easily imagine myself in Times Square on New Year's Eve or at Yankee Stadium just before game time. But when I began to listen to the sounds, to focus my attention so as to understand those voices, I knew I was very much in another country. In fact, I had the feeling I was in more than one country, for the voices I heard (I was to find out) came from such diverse places as Holland, Belgium, Luxembourg, Switzerland, Algeria, Morocco, Egypt, Dakar, Trinidad, and Denmark.

All streets in Lourdes, as one *gendarme* tried to explain to me, lead directly to the Sanctuary of Our Lady. A few minutes later I found myself standing outside St. Michael's entrance to the Sanctuary, searching in vain for the volunteer hostel. *"Où est l'Hospitalite de Notre Dame de Lourdes?"* I blurted out to several passing pilgrims. They nodded uncomprehendingly and passed by.

At that moment I noticed a white-haired man with a friendly face. I went up to him and repeated my question, *"Où est l'Hospitalite de Notre Dame de Lourdes?"*

"What is your native language?" the man asked me in French. When I was unable to reply he immediately assured me, "Ah, don't worry—I speak English. Please speak slowly and I will understand."

I proceeded to speak slowly, in carefully pronounced English words. Monsieur watched my lips, at the same time saying, "Oui, oui," but I wasn't sure at all whether he understood me. When he spoke in English I found it difficult to understand him. At least twenty minutes passed before either of us understood a word of what the other was saying. I must say, Monsieur loved to talk, and that was the trouble. His English, probably slightly better than my French, tried to express situations that even one with a surer grasp of the language would have found challenging.

His name was Eduoard. The retired army officer was courtly and Old World in his ways. I had travelled three thousand miles that day, and wanted nothing so much as a hot dinner and warm bed, but I waited patiently for him to finish talking. I didn't have the heart to say, "Monsieur, I would appreciate it if you would direct me to the l'Hospitalite de Notre Dame."

And so Monsieur went on with his good-natured monologue. The long pauses he took between each uttered word were beginning to panic me. Again and again he reached into the lexicon of his memory for the right English word, which had so eroded from lack of use that it came out of his mouth virtually unrecognizable. He used the pauses to apologize in French for his bad English.

The sun was beginning to set, the shadows to lengthen across the square, and I became afraid I would be stranded the whole night without finding a place to stay. Finally I said, "Monsieur, Monsieur." I must have sounded worried. Monsieur became silent. I explained with more haste than precision that I had come from the United States to serve as a *brancardier*, and I would appreciate it if he would direct me to the Bureau de l'Hospitalite de Notre-Dame de Lourdes, the volunteer headquarters.

When he realized what I wanted he practically exploded with delight, and revealed that he was himself a stretcher-bearer. To my amazement, his enthusiasm freed his tongue to speak more eloquently than I would have thought possible. "Ah," he pointed out, "there is no better man, no man possessing more honor and integrity than the *brancardier*. There is no work greater than he does. After all, he serves the children of the Mother of God. What greater honor?" He tapped my shoulder as if to say I had quite a bit to live up to.

At last he led me through the St. Michael's entrance of the Sanctuary to the Bureau des Brancardiers, which turned out to be a mere stone's throw away from where we had been standing for nearly an hour. Inside the building Monsieur Eduoard introduced me to the president of the Bureau, a blue-eyed, fair-skinned little man wearing a beret. I learned he was a count, a descendent of one of France's most illustrious families. As Monsieur Eduoard spoke to him about me, the count looked me over. Although Monsieur talked with gestures as if he were explaining the battle plan of Verdun, he was probably telling him what I had just told him a few minutes ago. I managed to make out exactly one word, *"Americain."*

While Monsieur talked on and on, the count quietly turned to the man standing next to him and whispered something. The man went over and opened a closet door, returning with a pair of leather straps called *bretelles,* which is the official badge of the *brancardier.* These are placed over the shoulders during work hours. The count brusquely interrupted Monsieur Eduoard's monologue. Nodding at me, he asked something I did not catch. Looking somewhat flustered, Monsieur translated what the count had said: "Do you have a letter of reference from his parish priest?" I shook my head. "Ah," said the count, looking to Monsieur to translate, "tell him he can work, but he has to write his parish priest for a letter of reference. Be here tomorrow morning at six. Good luck." The man who had gotten the leather straps put them on me, to show how I should wear them.

Once outside the volunteer headquarters, Monsieur Eduoard suggested I get a map of Lourdes. He then couldn't resist telling me why I needed a map, an undertaking that took him into further verbal difficulties. I listened with growing impatience. In the meantime the sun had set, and the day was rapidly changing to twilight. It was about 8:30, and I was burning to get away from Monsieur Eduoard. Since I was unable then to stay at St. Michel Abri, a barracks-like shelter where the volunteers ate and slept, located within Our Lady's Sanctuary, my concern was finding a hotel.

Monsieur eventually helped me to find one. He was a charming and kindhearted man. He was also lonely. "Ah," he said, after he had been talking a good fifteen minutes, "I know what you want, and I know where to take you." We walked slowly, with Monsieur talking the whole way, out of the Sanctuary and back into the town of Lourdes. In a little while we were standing in the lobby of the Hotel Alexander. He introduced me to the owner, a man named Jean, and proceeded to explain with great flourish what I wanted. The owner Jean assured me that he had a room, and I was so relieved that although I hadn't seen the room, I agreed to take it. Promptly I signed the hotel register and was given a key.

Monsieur asked me if everything was to my satisfaction. I said yes, and walked him to the door of the hotel intending to say good night. But Monsieur Eduoard decided to give me a summing up of the entire evening from the moment we met. He had been talking about five minutes when, suddenly, he said, "You will send me a postcard when you are back in the United States?" Touched by his request, I said, "I would be delighted to send you a postcard, Monsieur." He wrote his address in my pocket notebook. We shook hands. Monsieur was a thoroughly decent man.

In the Letter to the Romans (12:10, 13), St. Paul teaches that we should "love each other as much as brothers should, and have a profound respect for each other... and you should make hospitality your special care." In this sense, hospitality doesn't only mean how we treat our guests in our home. It is a habit of mind, a matter of paying attention to the presence of God in a stranger, of treating one another with sympathy and generosity, with insight and empathy.

Lord, help me to see my neighbor as someone always in need of love.

CHAPTER TWO

The Algerian Policeman

June 30. His name was Monsieur Rene Douffiague. He stepped into the restaurant of the Hotel Alexander during the busy lunch hour and, seeing me at my table, came over and said, "May I join you?" I looked at him. He wore a beret, and was probably in his middle fifties. "Sure." I offered him a seat. The minute he sat down he began to talk. He not only gave me his name, he taught me how to pronounce it: "Doo-FEE-ah-gay."

Monsieur Douffiague was a retired Algerian policeman. His 25-year stint with the French police happily behind him, what he was doing at the present moment was a gift from heaven. He lived in Lourdes for most of the year; the rest of the time he lived in Paris. He spent his time writing articles about the visiting pilgrims he had the good fortune to meet; he also corresponded with those pilgrims, mostly sick ones, whom he had befriended.

We had been talking only a few minutes when Monsieur Douffiague told me his wife had been a mental patient for twenty-eight years. He had to spend time with her, he explained, but didn't have to be with her *all* the time. I wondered why he should have taken the trouble to tell me this. But after listening to him I began to see what he was driving at.

"Ah," he said, "no one nowadays says very much about the

cross. You see, everyone complains about his rights, human rights, if you will, and everyone is entitled to them. Of course, of course. But I hear very little said about the cross we must carry. You see, without the cross we have no resurrection. We should think about this. You see, in Lourdes, everywhere you go, the contradiction of the cross is made manifest: here love and suffering and joy come together in an amazing way."

He was served a sandwich, but did not eat it. Monsieur seemed to want to talk only about Lourdes. Nothing, he said, made him happier than spending his days at Lourdes. His joy and his peace were Lourdes. He could not bear to be away for even a day. When he did leave, as was sometimes required, he felt exiled until he returned. He described Lourdes as not of this world: indeed, something heavenly envelopes it. As nowhere else, he said, gesturing with his hands, Lourdes has a climate of love.

Thanks to the Blessed Mother, one could not help being touched by the beautiful people one saw here, said Monsieur Douffiague. He knew many patients cured of their diseases, and many more cured of inner sickness, inner turmoil. It occurred to me to ask him whether he had brought his wife to Lourdes to be cured. I never got the chance. Abruptly he excused himself, explaining he saw a friend at another table. He got up, again excusing himself, went over and seated himself opposite a woman several tables away.

I was to see Monsieur Douffiague several times more, and each time I saw him I learned something. Since he spoke English well, I had no trouble conversing with him. I could see he was a person of strong commitment, and I told him so. "Ah," he said, "it is the least I can do. Besides, it is a requirement of our faith. We must all take a more active part in the work of evangelizing the world." He took out of his pocket a frayed copy of the Second Vatican Council documents, flipped the pages, and began translating from the French: "'The laity, too, share in the priestly, prophetic, and royal office of Christ and therefore have their own role to play in the mission of the whole People of God in the Church and in the world.'[1]

"All of us have the perfect role model in the Blessed Virgin Mary. Listen to what the Second Council says about her: 'The perfect example of this type of spiritual and apostolic life is the most Blessed Virgin Mary, Queen of Apostles. While leading on earth a life common to all men, one filled with family concerns and labors, she was always intimately united with her Son and cooperated in the work of the Savior in a manner altogether special.'"[2]

Monsieur Douffiague's faith in God and his absolute acceptance of the cross as the foundation of his faith was inspiring but also disturbing. "Precisely here," he said, "is where suffering and sacrifice as a requirement of faith in Christ turns away a lot of people. As it says in the Gospel of John:

> Many of Jesus' followers turned back and would not go with him any more. So he asked the twelve disciples, "And you—would you also like to leave?"   JOHN 6:66-68

"Ah," Monsieur went on. "does that surprise you? It happens every day. Jesus said other things hard to accept, such as, 'If you do not eat the flesh of the Son of Man and drink his blood, you will not have life in yourselves,' (Jn 6:53) What do you think he meant? He meant we will not have life if we are not crucified with him even unto death (of self). No wonder people turned away from him, and have been turning away from him for nearly two thousand years."

Later in the evening I met with Monsieur Douffiague again. Again he talked of the Virgin Mary. As usual he would begin by asking me how was I doing with my volunteer work, how was the work going at the train terminal, and so on. Any difficulties? Satisfied when I told him that all was well, he would begin his monologue.

"Ah," he said, warming up to what he really wanted to say, "who was this woman of Galilee? Was she a woman of influence and power? No. Did she have personal charm, a sparkling intellect, perhaps good looks? No, I do not think so. I see her as a plain woman, having plain ways. 'He (God) has remembered me, his lowly servant,' she says of herself. Paul scarcely mentions her. John, who took her to live in his home, cites her in his Gospel sparingly. Luke gives us more detail, but not much more.

"Mary would not have stood out in a crowd. She was lowly. Her husband Joseph worked with his hands. She did her work, she went to the temple. She was a hidden soul. A few who knew her discerned her greatness: Surely Joseph her husband did— Simeon, too, who predicted, 'sorrow, like a sharp sword, will break your own heart.' There was Anna who 'spoke about the child (Jesus) to all who were waiting for God to set Jerusalem free,' and Elizabeth her cousin who greeted her with the words, 'You are the most blessed of all women.'

"Yet what distinguished her from other pious women of Galilee, that God chose her to bear his son? The answer is innocence. I do not say naivete. My friend, she was not ignorant. She had an innocence which it is difficult (for us) to conceive: it was the innocence of wholeness, of the clear-eyed and clear-thinking, of the complete person. Mary was filled with the innocence of light: she stood the close scrutiny and presence of God at all times, she accepted all things, endured all things, because her strength came entirely from God. She did not escape suffering, but received her full share of it.

"She was a prefiguration of the New Creature of which Paul wrote in Ephesians 4:24: 'You must put on the new self, which is created in God's likeness, and reveals itself in the true life that is upright and holy.' She prefigures her Son in this true life. She was chosen by God precisely because she could be an example to her Son whose vocation was to be the perfect man. Mary helps bring this perfection out of him. She guides him through his boyhood and adolescence. For Mary has the likeness of God. But also like God she is hidden. We do not see her—we sense her, we discern the example she was to her Son. Indeed she is perfect in her likeness of God and in her hiddenness. But neither does she hesitate to act: 'Do what he says,' she tells the servants at the Cana wedding, and the miracle of turning water into wine is performed. She is the antithesis of Eve, the busybody Eve, who, looking for new thrills, new excitements, turns down a garden of love for a world of pain, disease, death.

"Not so Mary. In Mary, action and contemplation through God are made one. Everything she does has one spectator only, God. Her hiddenness rests entirely in God, for so God wanted it. And in God she has peace. But look at the things that were wrought through her! For when she says to the Angel, 'I am the Lord's servant, may it happen to me as you have said,' the saviour of the world is born, and victory over death becomes a possibility for all of us.

"Ah, my friend," said Monsieur, his eyes shining brightly, "we give thanks to the Virgin Mary to whom we owe so much, and always we ask for her prayers 'now and at the hour of our death.'"

Several days passed before I saw Monsieur Douffiague again. He seemed troubled. He explained that his wife had sent him a wire, asking him to return home. What, he asked with a touch of acerbity, could she possibly want from him now? He had just spent time with her a few weeks ago! I gathered from what he said that, although his wife was no longer seriously sick, she still conducted herself inappropriately, and that it was something of a trial to be around her. Again I thought of asking Monsieur whether his wife ever came with him to Lourdes. Again I stopped short.

My friend was now saying how glad he was that he didn't have to leave for Paris until morning. Ah well, he would worry about it in the morning. In the meantime he would treat himself to the Candlelight Procession that evening. At this I blurted out what I had wanted to ask him, "Did you ever bring Madame to Lourdes to be helped with her problem?"

We were seated at a table in the Hotel Alexander's restaurant. When I said this Monsieur looked startled, then lowered his eyes. For about a minute Monsieur Douffiague was silent, staring into his cup. He slowly raised his eyes and faced me. He said, "Ah, my friend, my wife does not believe in Lourdes, she does not believe in God, she does not believe in anything. I have been praying for her surrender to Christ for thirty years. I don't despair, but still, I fear for her, and I struggle with my impatience. I know my judging her, even to the smallest degree, sins against the charity of Christ."

After he had said this Monsieur Douffiague fell silent. Finally he said, "How wonderful it would be if every Catholic in the world could take part in Our Lady's Candlelight Procession. Why, I am sure the hearts of millions would be changed."

"Yes," I said, "it would be a wonderful thing."

*O Lord, help each of us to carry our cross,
looking to you for strength. Help us to respect
the hidden crosses others must carry, and to
resist the temptation to judge what is
behind what they do—or fail to do.*

CHAPTER THREE

The Way of the Cross

July 4. Calvary Hill, or The Way of the Cross, is situated on a hill overlooking Lourdes. The entrance is marked by a gateway, surmounted by an angel carrying a Cross with the inscription: *In Cruce Salus* (Cross of Salvation invites you). Pilgrims climb the stairs to Calvary Hill on their knees, whereupon they begin the first station of the cross, the one representing the condemnation of Jesus by Pontius Pilate. From prison, St. Paul wrote about this way of Jesus, the unfathomable depth of Jesus' love who "emptied himself and took the form of a slave... and obediently accepted even death, death on a cross!" (Phil 2:6-7).

That afternoon I did the steps with five or six other pilgrims. Once on top, I found myself rushing from one station to the next, as though I were in a museum looking at art objects rather than participating in one of the most honored of devotions of Roman Catholics. I passed the first station ("Jesus is condemned to death") and the second ("Jesus carries his cross") with almost unpardonable quickness, as if none of it had anything to do with me. I was gazing at the iron statue that comprised the third station ("Jesus falls the first time") when I was startled by a voice. I turned around to see who it was. He was a fellow pilgrim, a man of middle height, about thirty-five years old.

"I beg your pardon," I said. "But are you talking to me?"

"I'm just musing," he answered, without turning to look at me. We moved to the fourth station.

Fourth station: Jesus meets his mother. For several minutes we gazed at the Virgin Mary who, assisted by Mary Magdalene, meets her divine Son as he carries the cross.

The man spoke again. "Imagine having your mother watch you as you are being executed." My neighbor pilgrim had an English accent.

"It's not something I would like to imagine," I answered.

The man stood quietly before the huge figures. Then he turned to me. "The Way of the Cross is an ancient Catholic devotion—seventh century, I believe." He went on to explain that the Stations were essentially "a series of icons that mirrored the Way, the Truth, the Life of the inner human process in Christ Jesus."

Fifth station: Simon helps Jesus. When we reached the fifth station I commented on the figure of Simon the Cyrenian. I wondered aloud whether the artist was deliberate in showing a reluctant Simon helping Jesus carry his cross.

"Oh," said my guide, "very deliberate. The Roman soldiers compelled Simon the Cyrenian to help Jesus, lest Jesus fall again and further delay execution. Indeed, they wanted to be done with it. Mark 15:21 records soldiers forcing Simon to carry Jesus' cross. A similar incident is recorded in Luke 23, beginning with verse 26. Simon was dragooned by the Roman soldiers to help Jesus.

"Of course, Simon is like most of us," he acknowledged, smiling, "We have to be commandeered to be kind to one another. We must be constantly exhorted, cajoled, wheedled, commanded, threatened (even by hell fire) to help the suffering Christ."

Sixth station: Veronica wipes the face of Jesus. By the time we reached the sixth station I learned my fellow pilgrim's name, Samuel. I was on the point of asking him whether he was a teacher or possibly a priest. But at the sixth station he stood gazing so quietly at the kneeling Veronica with Jesus approaching her, carrying his cross, that I said nothing. Some doubt the veracity of the story of Veronica drying the sweat from the face of Jesus, and the bloody image of the holy face appearing on her linen veil. I wondered what Samuel thought.

"I wonder if she really existed," I said aloud.

"Oh, I believe so." My friend gave a quick run-down on the possibilities. "As you know, she isn't in the Gospels. She might be the wife of a Roman soldier, she might be the wife of Zachaeus with whom Jesus dined, she might be the daughter of the woman of Canaan. The earliest version, I believe, dated from the 4th or 5th century, identifies Veronica as the woman in chapter 9 of Matthew's Gospel."

Later I turned to the ninth chapter of Matthew and read:

As they [Jesus and the disciples] were going, a woman who had suffered hemorrhages for twelve years came up behind him and touched the hem of his garment. "If only I can touch his cloak," she thought, "I shall get well." Jesus turned around and saw her and said, "Courage, daughter! Your faith has restored you to health." That very moment the woman got well. MATTHEW 9:20-22

Seventh station: Jesus falls the second time. "The seventh station," said Samuel, as we came up to it, "is the epitome of humiliation. Jesus not only falls for the second time, he is ridiculed and taunted by his enemies. In life we all fall, and at some point we all pass through failure and ridicule. It is part of our inner journey to God. It is required."

Eighth station: Jesus meets the women. As we stood before the eighth station, Samuel shook his head. "Try to put yourself in Jesus' place. Would you be able to say as you faced torture and death, 'Daughters of Jerusalem, do not weep for me. Weep for yourselves and for your children'?"

I shook my head, "I don't think so."

"Neither could I," he admitted, "unless you had something very special..." He hesitated, then said, "As I see it, holiness transcends one's personal identity. In holiness we become like God. You see, for love of your neighbor, you become that neighbor in all that he suffers. That is what Christ did for us, and that is what Christ does for us today.

"Astonishing though it is, we have this holiness insight and holiness strength at our disposal whenever we ask it of God. This is what the eighth station tells me."

Ninth station: Jesus falls again. Samuel stood riveted, looking at the figures. "Here is where the Man-God hits rock-bottom, he fulfills the prophecy of Psalms 22:7-8. Do you remember these awful words? 'I am a worm, not a man; the scorn of men, despised by the people. All who see me scoff at me; they mock me with parted lips, they wag their heads.' Imagine doing something for love of somebody and having that somebody vilify you for it. It's no fun being hurt by people you love."

My guide stood a long time looking at the fallen Jesus. He seemed completely to have forgotten me. Abruptly he turned and strode over to the tenth station of the cross. I followed him.

Tenth station: Jesus is stripped of his clothes. "'They divided his garments, rolling dice for them'" (Lk 23:34), Samuel quoted. "How often have we rolled dice with one another in cynical indifference to our neighbor's suffering?"

Eleventh station: Jesus is crucified. The statuary figures stand around Jesus as he lies on the ground, a Roman soldier hammering nails into his hands and feet.

Samuel looked at me. "Try to imagine yourself that Roman soldier. You are holding the hand of Jesus on the wood and banging a nail into it. Could you have done it? Imagine seeing your brother, whom you have loved from the beginning, driving the nails into your hands and feet. You see, that is what we do every time we fail to love the Christ in our neighbor."

Twelfth station: Jesus dies. The twelfth station capsulizes the heart of the mystery of suffering in the words of Jesus. "Hear him say those terrible words," Samuel quoted, "'My God, my God, why have you forsaken me?' (Mt 27:46). There's the rub. When things go badly, we ask these words.

"But when Jesus says these words—actually he is quoting the beginning words in Psalm 22—he is prophesying himself. Jesus is saying in effect that what Psalm 22 speaks about is at that moment happening through him. Indeed, consistent to the end, faithful to his ministry, with his physical and spiritual agony at an apex, Jesus forgives the people who put him on the cross, the people whom he has loved from the beginning, the people whom he has never abandoned. For, you know, these people are ourselves. 'Forgive them, Father,' we hear him say, 'for they know not what they do.' Even to this day we know not what we do, with far less excuse than the people of his time."

Thirteenth station: The body of Jesus is taken down from the cross. I followed Samuel to the place where Jesus has been taken down from the cross by Joseph of Arimathea, placed in his mother's arms, while Mary Magdalene, kneeling, kisses his hand.

For several minutes we both stood looking at the figures in

silence. Suddenly I felt my throat tighten and tears filled my eyes. I kept on looking straight ahead, trying to get hold of myself. I didn't dare look at my pilgrim friend lest he should see me.

Fourteenth station: The body of Jesus is put in the tomb. By the time we moved on to the final Station of the Way, showing Joseph of Arimathea, Nicodemus, and St. John carrying the body of Jesus into the cave, I felt I had passed through an extraordinary experience. Again Samuel and I stood silent for several minutes. Then he turned to me and said, "It was nice we did this together." We shook hands and parted.

Next day at St. Michel's. A day later, I saw Samuel again as I walked into the small chapel St. Michel to attend Mass. The ordinary-looking man who gently invited me to do the Way of the Cross with him was an English priest from Cambridge. Father Samuel was wearing vestments and obviously was preparing to say Mass. I waved to him. He waved back, smiling. I suppose I wasn't surprised to see that he was a priest.

The Gospel that day was the story of Jesus casting demons out of two men (Mt 8:28-34). The two men came out of burial caves, which suggests that they lived as cast-offs, probably rejected by the townspeople because, as Matthew's Gospel says, they were so fierce that no one dared go near them. When Jesus meets the two men the demons in them beg Jesus to let them pass into the herd of swine. Jesus grants them their wish: "Go." The demons go out of the men and pass into the swine, which rush down the side of the cliff into the lake and are drowned. When the townspeople heard of this they implored Jesus to leave them. The townspeople were more concerned over the loss of their pigs than they were happy over the healing of the two sick men.

"The world often cares more about preserving its property and wealth than about the needs of the poor, the hungry, and the sick," added Father Samuel. "They will even support and promote war in order to vouchsafe what they have."

After Mass I went to Father Samuel to thank him not only for his wonderful Mass but for sharing with me his thoughts and insights on the Way of the Cross. I learned that he and his Cambridge students were leaving Lourdes the next day by minibus for their three-day journey back to England.

O Lord, I give thanks to you for persons like Father Samuel, who are crucial in helping us to understand the depth of your love for us. We need each other's help in our journey to you, and we are grateful to you when that help comes in a wonderful variety of ways.

CHAPTER FOUR

Fernand the Stretcher-Bearer

July 5. At the train terminal, when I first saw him pushing a patient in a wheelchair, I thought Fernand was putting on an act for somebody. If anybody belonged in a wheelchair, he did. Fernand wore spectacles and a beard, he was short and he limped; his legs in fact were bent at the shinbone.

As it turned out, Fernand didn't belong in a wheelchair, and he wasn't putting on an act. He was a certified Notre Dame de Lourdes volunteer stretcher-bearer. Indeed, as I was to find out, he was one of the best.

I watched him work, fascinated. How he kept his balance, how he managed to push those steel blue chairs, lift the patients out of the wheelchairs, and set them gently down on stretchers—hard work even with no physical disability—was a mystery.

He moved, as well as I could see, in defiance of gravity. His bent, disjointed legs spun out from under him in a strange cock-of-the-walk movement; all the parts of those misshapen legs, joints, knee caps, shinbones, ankles, insteps somehow propelling him across the floor. With every step he appeared on the verge of losing balance and falling. But no; his bent shin-bone legs found the ground each time. Not once in the seven days I worked with him did I see him fall.

Fernand was of medium height, about 5 feet 8 or 9 inches, but his corrugate shin-bone robbed him of inches; he carried himself with such taut energy and stiff-necked assurance, however, that he seemed taller than he really was. He was wiry, with long sinewy arms, strong hands, and thick fingers. He had a broad back and a small waist. He had an ordinary face. I would not have noticed him if he hadn't been handicapped. He was not sociable and spoke only when spoken to. During periods when the men weren't working, he stood apart. No one paid him any attention, though we spent hours working side by side with each other.

Many times during work, which was sometimes grueling, fellow Frenchmen would yell out cheerily to one another: *"Ça va?"* ("Everything okay?") But no one ever said anything to Fernand. And Fernand in his turn never said anything. He would come, he would go, like a shadow. After the initial shock of seeing this severely handicapped man wheeling patients around, I stopped noticing him.

One Friday night I had an opportunity to learn something about Fernand. We had started work at the train terminal at six o'clock in the morning; it was now nine thirty at night and we were still at it. We had worked all day, except for a ten-minute break in the morning and ten minutes in the afternoon. Hundreds of patients passed through our hands. By nine thirty we were exhausted.

We stood on the platform of the big station house, limp with weariness. But it wasn't over yet. The next contingent of sick pilgrims were expected to arrive from the Notre Dame Hospital located inside the Sanctuary itself. This meant two hours or more of work in hot, stuffy, smelly ambulance cars. In these cars the men worked hardest.

Fernand had spent most of the day working in one of these cars. In the corner of my eye, I had seen him shouldering his burden, his hands gripping stretcher handles. Back and forth he went, holding his end of the stretcher with his dead-weight patient. I knew it was hard going for him; it was hard going for all of us. This night was particularly muggy, particularly close, and breathing was difficult.

At last the sick pilgrims arrived from the hospital. We saw the lights in the cars hadn't been turned on, but we started work anyway. We worked in narrow passageways with barely enough light to see, all the time bumping and falling against each other. It was no fun for the sick being carried in, either; they depended on us to get them in the car and settled without mishap.

As usual we were organized in teams of seven; three men worked on the platform outside, four men inside the cars. The men from the outside lifted and handed over each patient to the men working inside the cars. The inside men carried the patient on a stretcher through the long, dark passageway of the car, found the bed or bunk and settled the patient inside it.

Fernand was content to work the inside of the cars. Again I marvelled. How he managed in those narrow, close quarters, lifting severely handicapped patients around—especially when he had to lift incredibly heavy, sick-bloated patients to the upper bunk in an ambulance car—is beyond explaining. It was hard enough for even a man of exceptional strength to do this kind of lifting.

On this night, however, Fernand must have shown signs of weariness. Perhaps he stumbled once too often, for I heard a few of the men grumble, "Why don't you take a rest?" or "Why not work on the outside? It's easier." Fernand ignored them and kept working. I saw the sweat running down his face and neck.

At this point I was called to work at the other end of the platform, and did not rejoin my team until about an hour later. As I was returning down the long platform, I was surprised to see Fernand standing slightly concealed behind a post. Beside him stood a tall man I recognized as a gentle Yugoslav I had come to know slightly. As I caught sight of Fernand, I was astonished. He was weeping. Tears were streaming down his cheeks. He kept lifting his rimless eyeglasses with his one hand while his other hand clutched a handkerchief which he brought down over his wet eyes.

The Yugoslav (I don't remember his name) shrugged. "He's hurt because the men told him to get off the team," he said in English, and added, "They're afraid he'll hurt himself or the patients." Fernand, who understood no English, kept saying, "I can do the work, I can do the work." The Yugoslav patted him on the shoulder. I, too, tried to comfort him, with my poor, broken French. "You'd best leave him alone," said the Yugoslav. "He'll get over it."

Fernand did get over it. A little later I asked Fernand if he would work with me. He said simply, "Oui." And so he and I worked a car together, carrying and lifting patients through the semi-dark, narrow passageways of the train. The tears had been wiped away. His brown eyes sparkled behind his spectacles. We took one stretcher after another from the hands of the other men. And all the while Fernand stood on those funny spinning legs of his, bending, backing away, lifting, the sweat pouring down his face and arms. He was happy. I felt good, too. God had touched us both.

Lord, thank you for the grace you give us to
overcome sadness and discouragement
when things go badly.

CHAPTER FIVE

Where Are You, Good Samaritan?

July 7. Clouds hung low over the Sanctuary, turning everything gray. Even the gorgeous flowers set around the statue of the Crowned Virgin appeared to droop and hang lifelessly. I was headed toward the Hospitalite, the headquarters for volunteer stretcher-bearers, to meet with Monsieur Paul. I was to assist him with assembling carriages that would carry sick pilgrims for the Procession of the Blessed Sacrament. Since rain threatened, the Procession was being held in the Underground Basilica, a vast structure big enough to hold 25,000 people.

As I walked off the Esplanade onto Rosary Square, I caught sight of Monsieur Paul standing just outside the Hospitalite, and I hastened toward him, but as I did so a man wearing dark glasses approached me.

"Please," he said with a strong English accent, "is there a lost and found department around here? I lost a pair of dark glasses and, you see," he pointed to the pair of dark glasses he had on, "the ones I'm wearing are not as good."

I pointed to the Bureau des Objets Trouvés (lost and found) just a few steps away. "Right there," I said. I turned to continue in the direction of Monsieur Paul, but before I could go the man spoke again.

"My eyes," he said, "can't take in too much light." I looked at the man more closely and noticed his face was badly disfigured. He had been in a terrible fire, he explained. Pointing to his face, he said, "I lost the sight of my eyes. But in 1968, on a visit to Lourdes with my mother, I received my sight again."

I patted him gently on the arm. "That's wonderful," I said. For the moment I forgot Monsieur Paul. I went with the man into the Bureau des Objets Trouvés a few steps away.

Inside, the woman shook her head; the dark glasses hadn't been turned in. She asked him to leave his name and address; she would notify him in case they turned up. "I shall be leaving tomorrow," he said, and added, "I hope someone turns them in by then."

"I hope so, too," I said. I was about to leave him—I had work to do. But the gentleman didn't seem to notice. He told me of his mother, who had passed away less than a year ago. It was the first time he had come to Lourdes without her. As he was saying all this I caught sight of Monsieur Paul scanning Rosary Square, as if he were looking for somebody. "Ah," I thought to myself, "he's looking for me. How shall I get away?" I had the awful urge to leave the man flat. I held on.

"No one knows what it's like to lose one's mother until it actually happens," he continued. He spoke in a soft voice, with a tone of almost childlike innocence. He seemed to have a great deal stored in himself, and he was letting it out to me as if he knew me. I listened but only on the edge of what he was saying, eager to be off to Monsieur Paul.

"Look," I broke in, "I've got to go to work now. You see, I'm a volunteer. It's great meeting you," I said. I shook hands with him and hurried away.

In the moment I had turned my eyes away Monsieur Paul had disappeared. I went into the Hospitalite to inquire. I was told the work of assembling the patients would not start for another half hour. "And where was Monsieur Paul?" I asked. The Hospitalite man shrugged.

I hurried back to where I had left the man with the dark glasses. He was nowhere in sight. Rosary Square teemed with pilgrims, priests, religious; how would I find him in such a crowd? I knew also that once everybody gathered in the Underground it would be impossible to find him. I returned to the Bureau des Objets Trouvés; I asked the woman if I could have the name and address of the gentleman who a few minutes ago had asked her about dark glasses he'd lost. I explained I had just met him and wanted to write to him. She turned around the big book: his name was Thomas Hopkins, and he lived in London. I jotted down his name and address and went out.

But throughout the work of assembling the sick pilgrims in the Underground Church, I thought about Mr. Hopkins. He remained in my thoughts even during the stirring invocations in which all that vast assembly supplicates itself before Almighty God: "Lord, save us, we perish! Lord, he whom you love is sick! Lord, that I may see! Lord, that I may hear! Lord, that I may walk!" Why was I so troubled?

The ceremony ended; crowds began pouring out of the Underground Church. I took my first sick pilgrim up the ramp, down along the Esplanade, back to the Asile Notre Dame (rest-house). The clouds had lowered even more, misting and wetting everything. I continued to think about Mr. Hopkins.

Clearly, I had failed him. Mr. Hopkins was lonely and full of grief; how sad that amongst all the statues and shrines and pilgrims and piety, he had found no one with whom he could talk. As for me, I'd had the chance to do what I should have done: I should have listened to him. I should have given him my complete attention and listened to him.

Lord, what would you have done if you were in my place? How would you have handled it? Would you have rushed off to do works of mercy when there was one to do right in front of you? I don't think so.

No, I did what the priest and Levite did in the story of the Good Samaritan. Perhaps the priest and Levite were on their way to do urgent business, perhaps they too had works of mercy to perform. Seeing only what their agenda told them to do, they ignored the man beaten and left for half-dead on the roadway. The Good Samaritan, too, had urgent business. But he let his business wait: He helped the man who needed his help. He dressed the man's wounds. He lifted him to his animal, took him to an inn, spent time there nursing him into the next day. He even told the innkeeper, "When I come back this way, I will pay you whatever else you spend on him" (Lk 10:35). Only then did the Samaritan go to do his other business.

Doing good does not conform to any rigid rule. On the contrary, doing good is creative, and springs from our personal freedom as human beings. Every good act is an act of creation, and stems from, imitates, and confirms God our creator. "God saw all he had made, and indeed it was very good" (Gn 1:25). All good things we do are inspired by God.

I hope Mr. Hopkins met that Good Samaritan before returning to his home in London....

Lord, help me to be like the Good Samaritan
who treated a stranger with neighborly,
compassionate concern for one reason only:
He was a person in need.

CHAPTER SIX

The Spanish Boy Scout

July 9. Pilgrims arriving at Lourdes from Spain keep to themselves; they don't mingle with other groups. Their pilgrimages are well organized and large, and they bring their own volunteers. The volunteers are outfitted like Boy Scouts in dark olive-green uniforms. I was surprised to see the Boy Scout uniform worn by grown men. At first I thought it a bit incongruous to serve God wearing uniforms with a military look, but then I thought better of it. What does it matter what we wear if it helps to put us in the right frame of mind to serve God and our fellow man?

The Spanish pilgrimages of volunteers, as I have said, do not usually socialize with volunteers from other nations. One evening a group of them, sitting by themselves at the back of the bus, were returning from a hard day's work at the train station. Suddenly they began to sing the "Battle Hymn of the Republic" at the top of their voices. I was startled when I heard it because I had associated this hymn with the American Civil War. Here it was being sung by Spaniards on the way to the Sanctuary of Our Lady.

Glory! Glory! Hallelujah!
Glory! Glory! Hallelujah!
Glory! Glory! Hallelujah!
His truth is marching on.

He is trampling out the vintage
    where the grapes of wrath are stored;
He has loosed the fateful lightning
    of his terrible swift sword;
His Truth is marching on.[1]

At the other end of the bus the French and the Italians took up the chorus: "Glory! Glory! Hallelujah!" Immediately the French and Italian voices were drowned out by the thunderous, ear-splitting roar of the Spanish. And when the words "His Truth is marching on" rang out again, I thought they were all going to draw swords and fall on each other.

Well, I thought, *so be it.* If they want to think that Christ's Truth is a battle cry, that is their affair. As for me, Love does not march, it does not wear hob-nailed boots, it does not shoot a gun, or drop a bomb.

"Behold," in the words of Solomon's Song, "he cometh leaping upon the mountains, skipping upon the hills." Love flies, or bounds among the eternities, or is nailed to the cross—but it does not march. Love is swift and no camera eye, certainly no human eye, can catch its moving. How does one catch a thing so delicate and fine, so bright and so invincible as Love? Only the human heart is given a glimpse of such moving.

I was privileged to glimpse such love in a middle-aged man from Spain who wore his ludicrous dark-green Boy Scout uniform. One rainy afternoon the 4:30 Procession of the Blessed Sacrament was re-scheduled in the Underground Basilica of St. Pius X because of bad weather. The basilica, situated a short distance from the Esplanade of the Sanctuary, was planned by a team of architects (Vago, Pinsard, Le Donne). It was consecrated on March 25, 1958, by the then Cardinal Roncelli, Archbishop of Venice, later Pope John XXIII. The acoustics within this structure tend to increase sound tenfold, especially when the organ is played. Hearing 10,000 singing voices, accompanied by the organ, in this place of mighty pillars and soaring arches is a moving experience.

On this bad-weather day the sick pilgrims were wheeled into the Church by volunteers and placed in rows around the High Altar of the underground Basilica. The Benediction of the Sick would be held without the elaborate out-of-doors Procession of the Blessed Sacrament, which normally took place on a daily basis. Instead, a concelebrated Mass (I counted twenty-four participating priests) was held at the High Altar under the sweeping arches of the Basilica.

During Mass one of the Spanish volunteers caught my attention, a man at least fifty years old who stood about six or seven rows ahead of me. He stood quietly in his olive-green uniform like a sentinel amid the assembled sick in their wheel chairs. I could easily have pictured him standing guard during a lull in battle or rushing against the enemy in a conquistadorial assault. His granite-hard face and thin lips drawn back in a smirk scarcely fit the description of the compassionate volunteer. I found myself wondering, *What could this warlike-looking man be doing in a place like Lourdes?*

Soon the Mass ended, and the singing of the Magnificat began. I was so taken up in the singing that I forgot all about the Spaniard. There was a pause in the singing while the Benediction of the Sick was invoked.

The invocations generate tremendous tension. Miracles have been known to take place at this point in the ceremony. Feelings run high, even among those of us who are not sick or handicapped. Indeed, one can only imagine what many of the sick pilgrims feel at this point of the ceremony—especially those who have been bedridden for years, those denied things that most of us take for granted. The hope that God will free them from their cross, will give them back their lives, is great indeed.

"Lord, I am not worthy to receive you, but only say the word and I shall be healed." The Sacred Host was lifted and everyone kneeled or bowed their heads.

Then it happened.

In the deep silence that followed the invocations, a woman seated in her wheelchair nearby suddenly bowed her head and began to cry. Her tearful sobs reached everyone around her. Fellow patients in carriages gazed at her sadly. Her weeping sounded like that of a little child instead of a grown woman. I wondered, *What could have moved this woman to weep as if her heart would break?*

Suddenly the granite-faced Spaniard, who was standing near the woman, leaned over and spoke to her. I could see his face from where I stood; the woman I saw only in profile. She had fine, delicate features, her hair combed straight back in a bun. As she continued to weep, I saw the Spaniard gently caress the woman's hair and cheeks. In that moment his stern countenance changed, and in its place I saw the depths of human concern. In this man's eyes I saw something of the divine pity, the face of Him who must see us in all our suffering frailties. How strange and mysterious is the human being in whom God implants the seed of his divine love. How wonderful when we see the flower of this love in such acts as this!

The woman stopped her crying and started to smile. A smile already played on the lips of the man, who now stood by the woman watchfully while the invocations to our Lord continued:

"Lord, if you will you can make me whole!"

As I watched, the stern look crept back into the man's face as he resumed his palace guard posture. No one would have dreamed the other face that it masked.

"O Mary, Mother of Jesus Christ,
Pray for us.
Comfort of the afflicted,
Pray for us."

CHAPTER SEVEN

Gianni

July 10. One day I was assigned by the Chief to work with the Italian pilgrimage from Bologna. This was my first encounter with northern Italians. They were robust, hearty men, and they loved to laugh. It surprised them that I, an American, would come all the way to Lourdes to work for nothing. Since I spoke little Italian it wasn't easy communicating with them. I did the best I could with the few Italian phrases I knew and by gesturing with my hands.

"Parlo Italiano un poco," I explained to Giuseppe, one of the pilgrimage volunteers from Bologna.

Giuseppe understood. He held up his hands to me and said (in Italian), "I know someone who speaks good English. Do you want to meet him?"

He had to repeat his question several times before I understood him. *"Si, si!"* I exclaimed delightedly. After weeks of struggling to communicate with my rudimentary French, I looked forward to meeting someone who spoke English.

The 4:30 P.M. Benediction for the Sick had just concluded. We *brancardiers* had begun wheeling patients out of Rosary Square. Although many sick pilgrims are installed in the hospice within the Sanctuary, the members of the Bologna pilgrimage, who were more severely handicapped than most, were settled in the Notre Dame Hospital. Located off Rue de la Grotte, this hospital had an elevator, a convenience that enabled us to attend to the needs of the pilgrims.

Giuseppe and I pushed the carriages carrying our patients through a thick mob of people, murmuring a polite, "Pardon, pardon" to everybody who got in our way. At last we arrived in the courtyard of the Notre Dame Hospital, and we left our patients in the care of other volunteers. Once we were inside the hospital lobby, Giuseppe told me to stand by the elevator. He would be right back with his friend.

Several minutes later I was tapped on the shoulder. When I turned around I was quite surprised by what I saw. Giuseppe's friend, a young man, lay in a box. The box, oblong in shape, had the look of a coffin on wheels. His friend lay back, his head on a pillow, his body covered with blankets. On closer examination, I saw the oblong-shaped box was only about three feet long. *He must not have any legs,* I thought. I noticed also that only one of the young man's hands, the left hand, was visible. The other, if there was one, lay under the blankets.

Giuseppe introduced his friend: "This is Gianni."

"How do you do?" Gianni said. His voice had a musical quality. Fair-skinned, blonde-haired, and blue-eyed, he couldn't have been more than twenty years old. His eyes were especially striking. They looked out in a blank stare. This puzzled me. I looked at Giuseppe to see what he might say: Giuseppe wore an impassive look.

"You speak English well," I said to Gianni, shaking his hand. He thanked me.

"Please speak English slowly so that I can understand you," he said in the same melodious voice. Again, I noticed his eyes looking out with a blank, meditative gaze. *How odd that he doesn't look at me*, I thought. After all, I was standing right in front of him. Finally I understood: He was blind.

He spoke English slowly (with a good accent), his voice throbbing with energy and excitement. Gianni was a ham radio enthusiast, and said that he frequently spoke with King Hussein (of Jordan), who was a very nice man. He struggled to describe his adventures with his ham radio, and gloated over the many friends he had made all over the world. He abruptly interrupted himself to ask me if I wanted to visit him in Bologna, and that he'd be happy to teach me Italian if I would help him with his English. He suddenly cried out, "I'm so happy! I'm so happy!"

Astonished, I looked at him: There was a ring of purest delight in his words. I tried to put myself in his place, but I couldn't. How could a boy with such a body, and blind too, be happy? I told him I would love to visit him in Bologna. We took each other's name and address.

The conversation turned to other things. Slowly dropping his words like musical notes, he explained how important it was to learn English, since all his ham radio contacts spoke it. He was full of things to say. But I found myself fidgeting. Gianni was, I think, too much for me to take in all at once. I interrupted him to explain I had to leave but would see him again tomorrow. I shook his hand and hurried away, his delighted "I'm so happy!" still ringing in my ears.

Once up the street, I regretted leaving him and wished I could have visited with him a bit longer, if only to give him a chance to practice his English. *Tomorrow*, I promised myself. Tomorrow I would visit with him and make up for the abrupt way I left him.

All the rest of the day I thought about Gianni. The more I thought about him, the more he baffled me. How, I wondered, could this warm, lovely spirit repose in such a deprived, truncated, crooked body? His wonderful eyes, though sightless, had seemed attentive, searching. Somehow you felt that he saw you very well with his spirit—he didn't need his eyes to see you.

Then I realized something else: Couldn't the same spirit that enabled him to "see" help others to see him, too? Couldn't it restore all the missing parts of Gianni and present him whole? The wholeness of his spirit made you feel as though you were looking at a normal, sighted Gianni with a strong, straight, healthy body, a Gianni with all the gladness of youth about him. His spirit peeped out, smiling from its quiet depths: a spirit playful, light, effervescent; a spirit free of all the grotesque limitations of the body. His spirit made you see the true Gianni.

Gianni was a paradox: He had every reason to be a profoundly unhappy human being. He was a young man deprived of everything but his one arm, a one-armed man embalmed in darkness.

Two days passed before I went in search of Gianni. Wandering in the lobby of the Notre Dame Hospital I met Guiseppe.

"Hi," I said, "how is Gianni?"

"Good," he answered.

"Where is he? Can I see him?"

"Oh, he'll be down shortly. We are taking him to the Procession." He opened the door and took the stairs up.

About ten minutes later, Guiseppe came off the elevator, wheeling Gianni. I stepped forward. "How are you, Gianni?"

"Hello, Steve," came the reply. Guiseppe said he had an errand to do and would be back at the end of the ceremony. Would I take Gianni to the Procession?

So off to Rosary Square Gianni and I went. At the Square, after taking our place with other sick pilgrims, we chatted and waited for the Procession to start. For some reason Gianni wasn't talking very much. He laid quietly with his head on the side of his pillow, his vacant blue eyes staring out. He seemed to be listening attentively to something.

A great crowd began filling the Square; people also gathered on the ramps and stairway leading to the Upper Basilica, called the Church of the Immaculate Conception. Hundreds of the sick were wheeled out and lined up in the Square. In a little while the priests and lay people would repeat these invocations:

> *Lord, have mercy on us!*
> *Our Lord, Jesus Christ, we hope in Thee.*
> *Our Lord, Jesus Christ, we love Thee.*

I looked at Gianni and thought how wonderful it would be if he could be healed and restored. Sick people are every day cured at Lourdes, sometimes people with serious diseases and handicaps. Of course, even in his broken state, Gianni modelled a wholeness in his spirit that captivated me. The spirit of God helped him to bear his suffering; it helped him to endure his broken body, his sightless eyes, his dependence on the kindness of other people. But how much better it would be if he were healed!

Surely, I thought, Jesus could cure Gianni, as he cured the lepers with their festering sores and hideous mutilations, cleansing and restoring them in a twinkling; as he cured the blind man who, after being touched by Jesus, was flooded with light, able to see the Jerusalem hills, the green fields, the gleaming skies of God's earth! One-third of Jesus' earthly ministry was devoted to healing wounded souls and curing sick bodies. Surely Jesus could touch Gianni now: Jesus could make him see, Jesus could restore his body, Jesus could have Gianni jumping out of that coffin box to dance and sing!

As I was thinking these things the invocations thundered out through the loud speaker over the vast assemblage of people.

> *Lord, make me to see!*
> *Lord, make me to hear!*
> *Lord, make me to walk!*

Soon thousands of voices chanted the "Gloria Patri." The Divine Praises followed in a powerful litany. Finally, the bishop who carried the Blessed Sacrament slowly passed by Gianni and myself. I stood kneeling with my head bowed, praying with all my heart for Gianni. The Procession carrying the monstrance passed hundreds of other sick pilgrims. In a little while the benediction ended.

I got up from my knees and looked at Gianni. Gianni had not changed—the same deformed body was lying in the little box. My prayers had not been answered. Did I really think Gianni would be miraculously restored? Did I really think I could move God with my prayers? The answer is hope, which is a gift of God, has us reaching for the impossible, and sometimes God, if he wills it, does make the impossible come true. At that moment, however, I felt I did not merit having my prayers answered, that I was not good enough.

Then Giuseppe appeared and the two of us wheeled Gianni through the thick crowds. Halfway to the hospital I heard Gianni burst out like a bird in song. "Oh, I'm so happy! I'm so happy!"

At the hospital I shook hands, first with Gianni, then with Guiseppe. I never saw Gianni again. The next day I was reassigned to work at the Lourdes train terminal. When I returned to the Notre Dame Hospital the following day, the Bologna pilgrimage had departed.

I was saddened to hear this, for I would have liked to say good-bye. I also wanted to thank Guiseppe for introducing me to Gianni, to thank Gianni for the miracle of being able to meet him through the loving spirit of Christ. But then, I suppose that saying good-bye wasn't absolutely essential, for in the love of Christ we never need fear departing from one another.

During the Procession two days before, we had all prayed so fervently for Jesus to heal Gianni. Although Gianni was not healed, Jesus did answer our prayers—not by giving us the miracle of a physical cure, but the miracle of a spiritual one. For no less miraculous than if Gianni had got to his feet and started dancing across Rosary Square were his absolutely astonishing words, "Oh, I'm so happy!"

> *Lord, you still give us your spirit in wonderful ways. Help us to open our eyes to your spirit, which reconciles everything to it—to love your spirit and to become one with it. Amen.*

Chapter Eight

How to Learn French in Lourdes

July 13. Alain was a small, young Frenchman who served with us as a *brancardier.* I think he came from Paris, for I detected city ways about him—quick, nervous ways, and he was pale. But I never found out for sure; my limited French prevented anything beyond the most rudimentary exchanges. I had to guess a lot about the people I met, a most unreliable pastime.

Alain's appearance was most distinctive. His face looked old, though he couldn't have been more than twenty-three years old. He reminded me of the French poet Francois Villon (who, as legend has it, was hanged as a thief and murderer). Seeing Alain going into the Grotto late at night, a huge pair of Rosary beads swinging at his side, would discourage any such comparison.

The resemblance was a purely physical one. According to a woodcut I saw of the profile of Villon, he had a hooked nose, and so did Alain. But this man, who entered the Grotto to pray, to be lost in the shadows with other praying pilgrims, certainly had nothing else in common with the poet-rogue Villon.

Was Alain a saint? No. Alain had a sharp tongue, and he sometimes used it on me. Once he saw how inadequate my French was, he teased me. It wasn't nice of him, but everyone has his own way, I guess. I found it difficult to cope with joking delivered in a language I didn't understand. I therefore gave everything Alain said the worst interpretation because what he said drew laughter from the men. This offended me. After all, nobody likes to be laughed at. Alain didn't seem to notice how annoyed I was. He was too busy telling his jokes.

Alain teased me in the morning on the way to the train station and on the way back in the evening, at the end of the day's work, he did the same. He shouted across to me (speaking in French, of course) in a bus crowded with volunteer men, "Have you mastered your French yet?" Loud guffaws filled the air.

He said other things in rapid, staccato French. More laughter. I squirmed in my seat. Suddenly I imagined myself rushing at the fellow, grabbing him by the shoulders, and shaking him. I shook my head—*no, that wouldn't do, not in Lourdes...*

Every morning, as the men gathered by the buses that took us to work, Alain came over to shake my hand. Now it happens that shaking hands is a French custom and done every time Frenchmen come together. Thus every morning Frenchmen methodically made the rounds going from one man to another. It didn't matter whether you were French or not, everyone's hand was worth shaking. Alain faithfully made his rounds, too. When he came to me he always had something to say, in French. He said it slowly, carefully pronouncing each syllable. He said, *"Vous comprendez?"* ("Do you understand?") If I said, *"Oui,"* he seemed pleased—if I said, *"Non,"* he frowned and walked away.

"He is stupid and rude," I thought to myself. But the next day I bought a French grammar book. I looked over the chapter headings—third conjugations, reflexive verbs, the imperfect tense—and gritted my teeth.

Next morning when Alain came to shake my hand, I blurted out, "Do you speak English—eh, smart guy?" I must have glared at him. He looked surprised. I added spitefully, "You might take the trouble to learn English—it's a two-way street, you know." Alain simply walked away.

I was late getting to the Sanctuary the next morning, and I missed the hand-shaking ceremony. The men were already gathered for morning prayer. *"Je vous salue Marie..."* In a few minutes we were hard at work, wheeling around patients from Belgium, Rome, Metz. It was a hot day: Sweat ran down our faces and backs.

The day finally came to an end; we were done, we could go home. We stood there, about fifty or sixty of us, sweaty and exhausted. In a few minutes we'd all be leaving to go to supper; some would be leaving the next day to go home, so a few of the men were saying good-bye to one another. Alain breezed by me (I had not seen him all morning) and I distinctly heard him say, in English, "I love you." I turned to make sure I wasn't hearing things. Sure enough, it was Alain. But he was gone, lost in the crowd.

That night I saw him again—he didn't see me—walking in his breezy manner, holding his huge Rosary beads. I watched him pass down the Esplanade, then turn and disappear among hundreds of pilgrims. I wondered about him and the ways of people. The words of a psalm came to mind. "What is man that you should be mindful of him, O God?" I have not, of course, figured out an answer to that question, nor do I expect I shall have the answer tomorrow. What is man? Only God knows.

The next day I didn't see Alain, nor the next. He had gone home. Bless him.

Lord, you said: "Do not keep judging according to appearances; let your judgment be according to what is right" (Jn 7:24). Help me then not to make snap judgments about my neighbor; help me to see him according to what is right.

CHAPTER NINE

Our Citizenship in Heaven

July 14. The 8:30 evening Torchlight Procession was drawing to a close. The pilgrims, stepping in solemn formation and holding lighted candles, were making the turn onto the Esplanade, led by placard bearers. As on every night, the pilgrims broke their formation as they crossed over into Rosary Square where, still holding half burnt-out candles, they gathered before Rosary Basilica to await final blessing by the priests.

On this night, as I started across the Square, I noticed the front lines of the procession were still moving forward, whereas the pilgrims in the back of the procession had begun dispersing. I stood flat-footed, not knowing which direction to take, whether to join the pilgrims at the point where they were breaking away or whether to keep with the procession still moving forward on the final loop of the Esplanade. I decided to stay with the procession.

As I caught up to the lines to get in step with them, a woman brusquely bumped me out of the line with her shoulder. *"Wir sind Deutsche,"* she said. ("We're Germans.") I tried to take the next slot in line; this woman too stiffened her shoulder to bar me from entering. Again I heard the words, *"Wir sind Deutsche."* I was angry, but I refused to be drawn into an argument with the women. I found another line where nationality was not placed ahead of Christian brotherhood and finished the procession.

The message of the fourteenth apparition of the Virgin Mary to Bernadette was clear: "I want people to come here in a procession." As I thought about the treatment I had received that night, I wondered what Mary must have thought of it. She didn't say, "I want Germans and Americans and Frenchmen to come here in a procession." After all, the procession is intended to highlight our Christian brotherhood. As St. Paul says in Galatians 3:28, "So there is no difference between Jews and Gentiles, between slaves and free men, between men and women: you are all one in union with Christ Jesus."

Alas, a nationalistic attitude among many Christians is far from passing away. Let me explain: As Christians we do nothing wrong in feeling affection for the ways and customs and language of the people of our own nation. We diverge from our Christianity, however, when we place our nation before love of God and people.

Let me touch once more on the meaning of the Torchlight Procession, as I interpret it through the words of the Virgin Mary. Having people come in procession means that region and country, language and culture, are to be set aside. Symbolically the procession is a movement, a journey, to reach that place for which all mankind is intended: the place where we are acknowledged as God's people, or, more precisely, as God's lovers. Here the task of the Church, which is to lead the people to the truth of Christ, has been accomplished. The Church can take credit for leading the people through the thorny paths of this life to the ultimate goal, to God. Arriving in Rosary Square all the people take pause; they have left the world behind in order to answer Christ, who has summoned them to the Father. Here all pilgrims stand with heads bowed before the Father. It is here the people receive God's blessing through the priests. The candles which have lighted the way are blown out. The Torchlight Procession has ended.

In obedience to Our Lady's command for people to come here in procession, we rehearse for the final shedding of our temporal citizenship, in preparation for receiving eternal citizenship in God's kingdom. The procession, beside being a corporal and spiritual act of homage to God and an honoring of Our Lady, signifies the end of the great scattering of the people of the earth, as told in the story of the tower of Babel (see Genesis 11).

The story tells of the birth of nations and the death of communication between the peoples of the earth. The story speaks of a people who had fallen so far away from God, whose perception of the spirit had been so cheapened that they thought they could build a tower reaching to heaven. In so doing, they were trying to achieve their own salvation!

Of course, they failed. The one language that bound them to the spirit of God was lost; thereafter the one people became peoples of many nations with tragic consequences. The climate of fear, distrust, and division between peoples—cut off from God and from each other—has gone on for thousands of years. The chance to restore the life-communicating spirit of God among all people, to become God's people with one language and one speech, was offered to the world by God himself through the person of his Son, Christ Jesus. Indeed, the day that his Holy Spirit descended on the disciples gathered in the Cenacle is the day of the re-birth of the world.

Pentecost is the sequel to the story of Babel. "All of us hear them (the Galileans) speaking in our own languages of the great things that God has done," said the people who gathered later to hear the apostles. Here the Holy Spirit, speaking through the lips of the Galileans, re-opened communication and the one voice of truth is heard by them all. God's language of love transcends the Babel of tongues that afflicted, confused, and divided men and women for so long.

These same people today gather in the Sanctuary of Our Lady of Lourdes, pilgrims from every place on earth: Dakar, Chicago, Kuwait, and Saskatchewan; Limerick, Copenhagen, Trinidad, and Afghanistan. The same Holy Spirit, the same language of love, God's language, is every moment of our lives offered to us. It is this language of love by which Jesus was able to say, "I have overcome the world."

Lord, may we learn to love each other
on earth as we shall in heaven.

CHAPTER TEN

A Poor Man Named Francis

July 16. One day I stood in the terminal house at Lourdes train station with about thirty other volunteer stretcher-bearers, waiting for a trainload of two hundred pilgrim patients to arrive from Metz. We had already done the preliminary work of placing pillows, blankets, stretchers, and wheelchairs behind the platform posts in readiness for the disembarking patients.

As I stood waiting a small, stooped man stepped out of the company of men and came toward me. I remember him smiling and holding his hand out. His name was Francis O'Hanlon. Francis was short, his face pinched with wrinkles and pock-marked. He smoked continuously. His thin, frail appearance suggested precarious health, and a big dent in the back of his head, as if something had once bashed him, somewhat distorted his appearance. Francis couldn't have been fifty years old, yet his wizened face and wrinkly throat and neck made him look older.

The moment he spoke I noticed there was something the matter with his speech. His thick Scottish brogue was difficult to follow because he seemed to chew his words before they were half out. I had to ask him to repeat himself several times. He smiled; apparently he was used to this. With difficulty I gathered why he had singled me out: He had learned I was from America and he wanted to meet a "Yank."

He labored to talk as I labored to listen until, a half hour later, the Metz train arrived with its two hundred pilgrim patients aboard. We all dispersed to begin our work. A long day lay ahead: Thousands of patients were to pass through our hands. Francis, who was small and frail-looking, threw himself into the work. I could see he didn't find it easy.

We gripped the heavy blue metal wheelchairs by the handles and tilted them so that the patients wouldn't have to drag their feet. Francis strained under the weight of these wheelchairs. I saw his knees buckle as he lifted stretchers with stomach-bloated patients. During these exertions Francis coughed and wheezed, which I later learned was due to his chain-smoking. His coughing and wheezing didn't stop him, though. Doggedly he kept pace with the other men.

That same morning trains from other parts of Europe arrived, each with their quota of pilgrim patients. In between incoming and outgoing trains, the men rested, talked, smoked, or rushed off for a quick cup of coffee. About mid-morning I encountered Francis again, wiping his brow as he saw me come up. As before, the words tumbled out so rapidly that I couldn't make them out. Patiently I listened to him: The jumbled sounds gradually decoded into intelligible messages.

Oh, how he loved Lourdes, he was saying, how happy it made him, how grateful he was to God for making it possible to spend his two-week vacation working in Lourdes, how wonderful of God to have allowed him to come to Lourdes every year for the past twenty-five years!

As the days passed I had the chance to observe Francis in different situations. What touched me about him was his need for friendship and how hard he sought it. Since the men took little notice of him, he didn't wait for them to come to him, rather he went to them. Sometimes the men pretended not to see or hear him. When he approached them, as I watched him do many times, he always came with his hand held out in salutation. The gesture made me think of a beggar seeking a handout. He would ask questions that no one took the trouble to answer, and made comments and observations that the men pretended not to hear. The men simply shied away from him because he was so difficult to understand. When someone to whom he had just said something looked through him as though he weren't there, Francis simply turned to someone else.

Sometimes he would find someone to listen to him. I watched him talking a mile a minute, puffing away at his cigarette and describing things every which way with his hands. The man would often leave abruptly and, undismayed, Francis would look for someone else. Eventually he would latch on to me. I liked him, but he grated on my nerves. His chatter was incessant, and half the time I pretended to understand only to keep him from repeating himself, which frustrated him and exhausted me. And yet this scarred, wizened, pock-marked, unprepossessing little man, who jangled my nerves every time he opened his mouth, always put me in good spirits. He reminded me a little of the saints we hear about who exuded goodness like an odor, spreading it about them like the dew of some heavenly cloud.

One night we finished work late, about ten thirty. The autobus unloaded us in the parking lot of the Sanctuary, near St. Michel's shelter house. It was a warm, humid night. A few of the men suggested having a beer at one of the sidewalk cafes and, Francis being from their own city of Glasgow, they invited him along. Francis looked surprised; he hesitated, then declined. One of the men mildly persisted. Francis shook his head, thanked him, and walked away.

An hour later, just as I came off Rosary Square, I noticed the stooped figure of Francis; he sat huddled in the shadows not far from the Grotto. His head was bowed and he was saying his Rosary beads. As I came abreast of him, I was about to hail him but his utter absorption stopped me. He seemed to have left the world, so engrossed was he in prayer. As I watched him I was struck by something I saw in his face. It was a look I have seen in the faces of hospital patients, patients who have endured long periods of confinement—months, even years, of lying in bed or sitting in hospital corridors; a look of utter stillness and resignation and waiting.

I couldn't help thinking: No one could pray as Francis did who had not endured much. Certainly his speech impediment must have caused him distress: I saw people rebuff him because they found his speech scarcely intelligible. I saw them walk away from him in the middle of something he was saying, leaving him standing there still moving his lips as if he were talking to himself. But if Francis suffered from loneliness and frustration brought on by his speech problem, there was one thing that seemed to overshadow his pain.

Jesus said it best: "Peace I leave with you; my own peace I give you. I do not give it to you as the world does. Do not be worried and upset; do not be afraid" (Jn 14:27). It was this peace that I saw in Francis.

On Francis's last night at Lourdes, the two of us agreed to meet at 11 o'clock by the statue of the Crowned Virgin for a last visit at the Grotto. We had met at the Grotto at night twice before, after a day's work, to pray and keep vigil together.

At 11 o'clock, as I came up the Esplanade, I noticed Francis already waiting for me. He stood under the statue in absolute stillness. His head was slightly askew, as if he were listening attentively to something. His Rosary beads hung loosely in his hands, and his lips were pursed in a flow of prayer. Watching him pray, it occurred to me that if Francis had difficulty communicating with people, he had no difficulty communicating with God. Surely God heard his every word and never asked him to repeat himself. For him "the feast of reason, and the flow of soul," as the poet Pope[1] has said, was entirely with God.

After sitting about twenty minutes in silence on the benches with other pilgrims, we got up and came before the white carrara marble statue of Our Lady set in the niche of rock above the entrance of the Grotto. The inscription below read: *"Que soy era Immaculada Counception,"* that is, "I am the Immaculate Conception."

I followed Francis into the Grotto. He walked slowly in, stood before the hallowed rock with his head bowed, praying, then he leaned forward and kissed its worn, dark surface. Suddenly he turned around and handed me a tiny religious locket and, in clearly pronounced words, said, "There's a relic of St. Bernadette's clothing inside it—keep it." I took it, moved.

We shook hands by the statue of the Crowned Virgin, then parted. I watched his small, stooped figure move slowly down the Esplanade in the direction of the volunteer shelter house.

Lord, help us to see and appreciate those who love you. Help us not to be deceived by appearances. Amen.

CHAPTER ELEVEN

The Odd Couple

July 17. I met Teresa and Henry at the Lourdes post office. I had been trying to put a call through to New York City. Teresa had been trying to reach Chicago. When I heard Henry and Teresa address the telephone girl at the desk I knew they were Americans. Overjoyed at hearing American voices, I went over and introduced myself. Soon we were talking to one another like old friends.

Teresa and Henry had planned to be in Lourdes only twenty-four hours. They had six days of their vacation left, and planned to go to Madrid, and from there to Portugal's Our Lady of Fatima Shrine. Then they would return home to Chicago, where Teresa and Henry worked for the same plastics company.

"You see," Teresa explained, with a trace of an accent I could not place, "we are friends."

"Yes, friends," echoed Henry. "And the hotel clerks are wondering why we take separate rooms." He shrugged as if there were something peculiar about such clerks. I looked at Henry. What he said took me by surprise. I wondered what he meant, but I didn't ask him.

The small post office room began filling with people of every nationality. To be heard we had to shout above the babble of foreign voices. Eventually our names were called out and we took our long distance calls. I had enjoyed our conversation so much that I offered a hasty invitation to meet them again that evening.

"Look," I said, "if you've nothing planned tonight would you like to take part in the Torchlight Procession? Starts at 8:30."

"What's that?" Henry asked.

I described it.

"We would love to go," Teresa said.

"Don't forget tonight," I called after them as we took leave of each other. I watched Henry and Teresa leave, arm in arm.

That evening we lighted our candles and joined in the recitation of the Rosary that the processionists had already begun. At the conclusion of the Rosary the lines of the Procession started moving in formation. Holding our candles, we began the procession slowly along the Esplanade des Processions which would take us to Rosary Square. While the lighted candles flowed out under the evening sky, the noble strains of the organ sounded. Then, with a single voice, the processionists began singing:

> *The Bells of the Angelus*
> *Are calling to pray,*
> *In sweet tones announcing*
> *The Sacred Ave.*
>
> *Ave, Ave, Ave Maria,*
> *Ave, Ave, Ave Maria.*[1]

Afterwards we stopped at La Gare Cafe for coffee. It was crowded with young French people beating the tables and singing at the top of their voices. We endured the racket for several mind-boggling minutes. I had the panicky feeling that everything around, including the roof, would break into a thousand pieces. Finally, without ordering our coffee, we fled.

In a quieter restaurant we sipped cafe au lait and chatted. Before long my friends broached the delicate subject that had been troubling them both. In plain words, they were caught between the wish to conduct themselves in accordance with their Christian training and the physical attraction they felt for each other.

I asked them what had made them decide to travel together. It turned out that Teresa and Henry had been given their vacation at the same time, and since both were planning to visit Europe, they decided they would travel together. Knowing the temptations they might encounter, Teresa and Henry solemnly agreed to keep their relationship spotlessly platonic.

They never dreamed, however, that taking separate rooms would attract the attention of so many hotel clerks. Wasn't their conduct proper and correct? Eventually they began to understand that they were attracting attention precisely *because* their conduct was proper and correct.

From hotel to hotel throughout Europe, it was the same story. Hotel clerks asked the same question: How could a young man and woman traveling together take separate rooms when one room would save them money? Teresa and Henry ignored such callused thriftiness: Each paid for and—what especially baffled hotel clerks—stayed in a separate room.

When they finished telling me about hotel clerks who found it so difficult to mind their own business, they fell silent. I could see they were waiting for me to say something. When I didn't, they asked me straight out what I thought about their predicament. I looked at both of them and honestly didn't know what to say.

I was sympathetic. It's not easy to walk the straight and narrow when you're young, especially when you happen to be on vacation together and, hardest of all, happen to like each other. On the other hand, wasn't their going on vacation together in the first place, even if their intentions were good, asking for trouble? But I didn't tell them what I was thinking.

Instead, I said I thought they were right to take separate rooms since it was in keeping with their Christian faith. I said I thought what they were doing was the right thing—and it didn't matter what incredulous hotel clerks thought about them. I assured them that, in the end, responsible conduct has its own reward and that they would not regret what they were doing. Teresa and Henry beamed at these words. I suspect I was the first person to offer them this encouragement since their arrival in Europe.

We had come out of the restaurant and headed toward Rue De La Grotte. The last stop of my somewhat improvised tour was a street called Rue Des Petite Fosses where Bernadette had lived with her family in dire poverty in a house called "Le Cachot" (the prison house). The room was so small that two persons holding hands could touch the walls on either side. How a family of six lived in such tiny quarters is hard to imagine. It was too late to visit the house, which is kept open for pilgrims by the Sisters of Charity.

We walked back to their hotel. In the morning Teresa and Henry would be leaving for Madrid. "Thanks for taking us around," Teresa said. She kissed me on the cheek. Then she went inside. Henry stayed on. He turned to me and said, "Can we take a walk?" I said, "Sure." We turned our steps toward the square in town.

We walked in silence. After a bit he said, "Look, there's a lot of things I don't understand. I mean I don't understand the Church's position on sex. Why is the Church so strict?

"Don't get me wrong," he added, "I accept the teachings of the Church, and I do what is expected of me, but I've never understood the Church's prohibitions against sex. I was wondering," he added shyly, "I mean, what do you think about it?"

I listened to Henry sympathetically. I understood what he was feeling. I had given the subject a great deal of thought. Still, I didn't know how I could put it to Henry. I didn't want to sound prudish. I decided I would answer him with a bit of overstatement.

I said, "Henry, are you suggesting that sex become an unrestricted practice—done with whomever you wish, at any time, without thinking of the consequences?"

"No," he said. "I didn't say that. Not with just anyone. But why not with someone whom you like?"

"Henry," I said (and I wasn't trying to be funny), "if I could have sex with all the women I like, I should be busy doing nothing else. Look, God made men and women attractive to each other. It is not wrong for men and women to be sexually attracted to one another. What the Church says is wrong, however, is to pursue a relationship with pleasure as the primary consideration. The Church's stand on sex is, I believe, sound and reasonable: Sex should be creative, it should lead to something—to love, to life, to growth. This clearly calls for a permanent commitment between a man and woman. In other words, marriage. Arbitrary sex is not something to build one's life upon."

"I agree with everything you say. But, you know, it's not easy to put into practice," Henry said. "Besides, Jesus never said half as much about sexual peccadilloes as he said about the greedy rich."

"What he said is that we should be perfect, Henry," I reminded him. "And if we are to be perfect, like God, we are to love like God. We become as the greedy rich when we place sexual gratification above love of the person, above a life of commitment with that person. When we don't we do enormous harm to one another. The journey through this life is a brief thing, Henry.

How nice to know that we did not hurt that girl or betray that spouse when we come before God. And all unrestrained sexual gratification is want of love."

"Oh I wouldn't hurt Teresa for the world," said Henry, and added, "Never."

We had already turned our steps back towards the hotel. At the hotel's door, we shook hands. "Good luck, Henry," I said.

He grinned, "Thanks for the tour."

> *Lord, help us to overcome the temptation to gratify ourselves at the expense of others. Help us to love one another as you love us. Amen.*

CHAPTER TWELVE

"The Tongue Is Like a Fire"

July 20. One night I was returning from the Torchlight Procession holding in my hand a half burned-out candle. Thinking I would have a cup of tea when I got home, I stopped in a bakery to buy a roll. As I walked in I heard the baker exclaim to his wife and daughter, "Here comes another sinner!" This was followed by uproarious laughter.

"Ah," I thought, squirming as I heard them laugh, "where's the joke?" I bought a few rolls and walked out. All the way home I heard their laughter and it bothered me.

In my room I sat and thought about it, and the more I thought the more I came up with reasons to disparage the baker and his family. I had been forewarned by visiting pilgrims to expect the worst from Lourdes townspeople, and I was coming to believe they were right. A few of these people, shopkeepers selling religious baubles and knick-knacks, were rude to me, one called me an idiot because he could not understand my French, and one cheated me. Yes, I was coming to agree with visiting pilgrims: The people of Lourdes were rude, cynical, avaricious—a species of petty crooks.

As it drew close to my bedtime, I switched from brooding to praying. But as I prayed I found myself feeling uneasy. "Lord, help me to see my fellow man..." My mind wandered; soon I found myself remembering my hasty impressions about the baker and his wife and daughter, shopkeepers whom I had regarded as mean-spirited. How could I say such things about people I had never actually met?

I felt uneasy, especially when I remembered the story Jesus told about the tax collector and the Pharisee (see Luke 18:10-14). The Pharisee considered himself to be a good man—certainly better than the tax collector. The tax collector, however, minced no words about himself, humbly admitting to God that he was a sinner. Jesus tells us that the tax collector was in the right with God; the Pharisee was not.

In Luke 15:2, Jesus was criticized by the scribes and Pharisees for eating with tax collectors and outcasts—as if the scribes and Pharisees were so perfect that they could afford to criticize Jesus. And in John 8:7, Jesus offered these words to the Teachers of the Law and the Pharisees about to stone the woman taken in adultery, "Whichever one of you who has committed no sin may throw the first stone at her."

As these thoughts accused me, I started pacing back and forth. Lord, I thought, where am I wrong? Tell me what is it that I don't see? The question I put to the Lord was rhetorical. I did not really need the Lord to tell me. I knew the answer, because the Lord had given me the answer many times before: It is wrong to judge people one does not know, it is wrong indeed to judge even people one presumes to know.

Here I was, judging the people of Lourdes based on listening to what foreigners said about them. I was letting people tell me what to think about people I did not know, I was listening and making a judgment based on rumor and gossip. I was judging and condemning a whole people based on a few bad experiences. I was doing what I have seen other people do: turning unsubstantiated rumor and hearsay into a dark vision, a principle, a policy. My thoughts were adding to the vast deposit of lies, slander, exaggerations, and recriminations we keep at hand and use against other people.

What would have happened if people had not listened to what other people said of their neighbor in places like Northern Ireland, the Middle East, Bosnia? What would have happened if they had objectively examined what the accusing sides said of one another, if they had sifted out the opposing points of view and isolated them in order to see them better? How often do we feed anger, rather than doing what we can to extinguish it? How much better to choose not revenge but forgiveness! How much easier the way of peace when we see the offending neighbor with the eye of God's charity!

By the time I finished my self-examination I saw the picture very differently. Going back over the incident of the evening I tried to put myself in the baker's place. I had to admit that the bakery people's laughter had been quite without malice. Baking and selling bread and cakes all day is hard work, and if you do it year in and year out it could become boring—a few jokes might go a long way to make time go by.

As I thought about it I was able to see things from an entirely different perspective: It is evening, and all day long the baker and his family have been baking and selling. They are tired, they are bored. Now at the end of a long day in walks this pilgrim foreigner (myself) holding a candle in his hand, looking (I hate to say it) the image of incongruous piety. "Here comes another sinner!" Uproarious laughter. Would I laugh if I were in their shoes? Yes.

The truth is, all generalizations—the pious pilgrim, the shady shopkeeper—are dehumanizing, for these assumptions prevent us from seeing the real person. As I became more familiar with some of the "locals," I was able to set aside my own assumptions in order to see things from their viewpoint.

For the townspeople, living in Lourdes would be much like

living on a movie set: Each day was the sameness of ceremonies and processions, the perpetual confusion caused by the thousands of nameless foreigners coming and going, the incessant babbling of foreign tongues. Under these conditions, it is understandable that the all-too-visible, holier-than-thou look of a well-dressed pilgrim foreigner might trigger either cynicism or, as in my case, uproarious laughter.

By the time I turned off the light to go to sleep that night I resolved to see each person as a new creation, worthy of respect if only because he or she is made in God's likeness. Having resolved this, having asked God to help me to see people with his eyes, I felt better, and I was able to go to sleep.

Lord, help me to listen to what you have to say about my neighbor. You will always say the truth and you will never deceive me about my neighbor. And what you have to say is kindly and sympathetic and forgiving. Help me always to see my neighbor in your light.

CHAPTER THIRTEEN

Father Ulrich and the Bigot

July 21. Father Ulrich, a priest from Munster, Germany, never exchanged fifty words with me, and yet he impressed me. It was not that he did extraordinary things, but that he did ordinary things outstandingly well.

Father Ulrich came to Lourdes with six of his students, boys of college age. They planned to spend eight days of their vacation working as volunteers; the rest of the time they planned to travel through southern France before returning to Munster. Father Ulrich was allowed to do volunteer work, provided that he replaced his clerical garb with layman's clothing. This was a rule of the Hospitalite de Notre Dame de Lourdes, and it was observed by all priests who wished to work.

And so, wearing a simple black turtleneck sweater, Father Ulrich led his high-spirited boys by his good example. He was so quiet a man that his boys overshadowed him.

I never heard him grumble. Whatever he was told to do, he did it, and the boys followed him. He tackled the work with the innocence of a man not used to heavy, manual work. He tried several times to lift patients without first thinking whether he was physically up to the task. Many times the Father's knees buckled under weight he had misjudged. Lifting patients seated in wheelchairs or patients lying on stretchers through the high windows of cars (with the help of another man) required a knack that this German priest did not possess. Poor Father Ulrich often lifted with his back instead of with his legs; I sometimes wondered how he managed to avoid hurting himself.

But Father Ulrich never complained. Of course, among severely handicapped people it would seem silly to bemoan our small inconveniences, but there are times that try everybody's patience. Trains are late and the volunteers wait for hours; work goes past the lunch hour; disagreements arise among volunteers on how best to handle a patient. Once I saw a patient laid out on a stretcher balanced precariously across the open window of a car; the two volunteers holding the stretcher at either end were arguing loudly on how best to put the patient through the open window. The patient, in the meantime, stared straight out, nervously holding on to the stretcher bars.

Although there were many good men and women among the volunteers, like Father Ulrich, there were times when human nature was all too evident. From time to time discussions could become quite heated. There were religious differences on how to understand the Catholic faith; there were various personality clashes and animosities among the volunteers. Here is where, I believe, Father Ulrich's patience was sorely tried.

To begin with, our particular work team—a seven-man team assigned to assist arriving and departing patients—consisted of Father Ulrich with three of his boys (his other three boys worked elsewhere), two young men from Glasgow, and myself. The young Scot named Hugh, age 22, was given charge of the group.

For reasons no one understood at the time, Hugh did not like Germans. He was a big strapping young man, and he ordered Father Ulrich and his boys around like children. Hugh found fault with the way they handled patients, though they were gentle and efficient, and probably better than a lot of the other volunteers. Hugh also found fault with their ability to comprehend English, and berated both priest and boys when they did not respond to his orders quickly enough, though both the priest and the boys understood more English than he understood German.

Once, after some particular discourtesy to Father Ulrich, Hugh said to me, "I would never talk that way to my own priest." I could scarcely believe my ears. Hugh was intelligent, with a college education, and, in addition, a believing Christian— how could he judge a fellow Christian based on his nationality?

It has been said that the greater one's perfection, the less one is noticed for it. Certainly that was true in Father Ulrich's case. I marvelled at the way the German priest took orders from Hugh, who was at least thirteen years his junior. Father Ulrich quietly went about, unobtrusively doing his job.

The boys followed the priest's lead, and Father Ulrich and his boys went on to finish their eight days of work. Not once did I see a trace of anger in Father Ulrich. He was always pleasant and attentive, both to the sick pilgrims and to fellow volunteers, and he always did what he was told to do in good grace. If others noticed the way Hugh ill-treated the German volunteers, no one said anything.

Many times I asked myself: What did Hugh have against the men? And why should he bully them? The story came out of Hugh during periods when work slackened and the men stood around doing nothing. It was not hard getting his story: He seemed to want to justify his rudeness.

Hugh's story was this. Shortly after Germany invaded Poland, on September 1, 1939, Hugh's father, a soldier in the Polish army, was captured by the Germans and spent several years in a concentration camp. He escaped and was recaptured; he escaped again, and made it. He reached England and fought with the Polish Liberation Army. Later his father learned that the war had claimed the life of his father, his two brothers, and other members of his family. Apparently Hugh's father never forgave this. After the war, his father married a Scottish girl, and they settled in Glasgow to raise a family. Hugh must have listened to his father tell stories about life in a concentration camp and, I suspect, came away with his father's view of Germans.

One night I saw Hugh and his friend, a fellow Scot, in a cafe. They were both drinking French beer, which happens to be pretty strong stuff, and both were singing at the top of their voices. It seemed incredible to me that he could be the same embittered young man who pushed Father Ulrich around and, on the whole, conducted himself like a prison guard. There he was singing lustily, looking light of heart. When he saw me passing down Rue de la Grotte he shouted to me to join them.

Did Father Ulrich see this in Hugh? I think he did. He certainly could not have failed to notice Hugh's bad manners, nor could Father's poor command of English have caused him to miss the sense of Hugh's jibes. However, it was precisely these jibes that Father Ulrich appeared not to notice.

On the last day we shook hands. As we gripped each other's hand we gave the other a knowing look. There was a twinkle in Father Ulrich's eye, as plain as day. One by one I shook hands with the boys. We wished each other God's blessing. The next day they were gone.

Several days later it was Hugh's turn to leave. I watched him go into the Grotto and kiss the rock, then bow his head and pray. He stood a lonely figure under the statue of the Virgin Mary. What was he thinking about? Did he see something of the paradox of being at a place hallowed for works of charity and his own not very charitable conduct?

I think I understood what tormented Hugh, what torments so many of us when we see those we love victims of injustice and violence. How hard it is to forgive our enemies, and not to strike back against them! How easy to continue the vendetta, even where nothing is gained except further hurt and misunderstanding. Sadly, we see this vendetta at work among people all over the world.

The path of love, alas, is booby-trapped and tortuous. That is why we need God to help us every step of the way.

Lord, keep us from passing on to our
children our hurts and hatreds
and prejudices—lest these attitudes,
through our children, spread to other people.
Help us to teach our children
the sanity of Christ's love and forgiveness.

CHAPTER FOURTEEN

Lucienne

July 29. I had been in Lourdes nearly a month. I stayed the first week at the Hotel Alexandra, then for nearly three weeks in a tiny matchbox of a room at the Hotel Aragnouet, which was situated near a spiral staircase. I was frequently jarred awake by the sounds of people climbing the stairs at all hours of the night.

The St. Sylve room was larger and, above all, quieter. The Belgian couple who ran the pension had lived in Lourdes for years; they were authentic Lourdes townspeople. They kept their pension open from March to October, and earned what they could during these busy months because the money had to last them the rest of the year. (What they did for a living in the off season, I never found out.) Fifteen-year-old Lucienne was their adopted daughter. Her sparkling smile charmed me, and soon we became friends.

In time I got to know the whole family. As a young girl, Lucienne's mother had spent about a year in Los Angeles working as a waitress. For some reason this big, hearty woman would dissolve into gales of laughter at the very mention of that city.

Lucienne's father had been in an accident; he limped and had scars on his face. Lucienne's uncle, her father's brother, was part of the family and sometimes waited on tables. Lucienne's mother also took care of her deceased sister's son, Pierre.

On several occasions, I went to eat at the restaurant and found all the tables empty. As I began to eat, Lucienne's father would limp in, notice the empty tables, then mutter under his breath as if it were all my fault that business was bad. I understood that this act of protest was not really directed against me, but it unnerved me nevertheless. When I first came I wondered why so few guests patronized their restaurant—the food was exceptionally good. After spending a day and a night, I understood why.

Lucienne's father scared them away! He was a rough, uncouth man. One never knew what he was going to do next. As customers sat dining, he would come in abruptly, glaring at us all, then limp around his restaurant, looking from face to face as if he were sizing us up. Suddenly his mood would change and he'd start waltzing with his huge, shaggy mongrel dog or carry on running monologues with his red-feathered parakeet.

It was embarrassing to watch him, though it was obvious that his horseplay was intended for the entertainment of his guests. The guests politely tolerated him, but were annoyed that he kept them from their soup. He annoyed me, too. After all, his place was a restaurant, not a cabaret.

A black cloud lay over this family; they were always quarreling, always in conflict, and I frequently became an unwilling spectator. Every day was a free-for-all, especially between husband and wife.

Here is what happened for the few minutes I sat in their restaurant each day; the husband came limping out of the kitchen after a screaming contest with his wife, looking neither left nor right. He came out muttering and groaning and cursing under his breath. He turned and began kicking his dog. The dog whined and whimpered and crawled away. A moment later the man came rushing back. He fell to his knees; then, his voice croaking with contrition, he begged for his dog's forgiveness.

During this pitiful display, the wife shouted at him from the kitchen. With a roar he rose and rushed into the kitchen. From the kitchen I could hear her voice rising above that of her husband's. She wasn't being physically abused by him: the violence was all verbal, and from what I gathered she gave as good as she got. Once during one particularly loud screaming contest accompanied by the sounds of clashing pots and pans, I remember getting up from the table at which I was eating and running out.

Another time I saw the brothers throw a man out. The man had been drinking wine with them and was greeted as a friend just moments before. The men were huddled conspiratorially, speaking in low tones over a glass of wine. The friend leaned backwards in his chair, slightly tilting it. In a twinkling I saw Lucienne's father kick the chair out from under the friend, who fell back, his arms flailing. A short struggle between the two men ensued.

Good paying customers who witnessed this scenario simply got up and walked out. I suspect many did not come back.

It wasn't long before I, too, had endured enough and began to seek out other quarters. However, I was reluctant to leave until I had secured another room.

I describe the above to show the kind of atmosphere the young girl Lucienne lived in: It wasn't exactly wholesome. Yet through all these scenes, Lucienne appeared calm and cheerful. She was always smiling, always gracious with her guests, even as her guests, listening to the crash of crockery in the kitchen, gritted their teeth. During some of the worst moments—and they took place, as I have said, just as I arrived to have dinner—she went about serving her guests, if there were any guests, quite as if nothing extraordinary was happening.

I would give her my order in my broken French. Just then her father would limp into the restaurant, take a look to see who was around. No one but me. Lucienne gently continued to wait on me, even as I kept half an eye on her father to see what crazy thing he would do next. He would place himself at the center of the room and appear to be in deep thought. Then he would mutter something, whirl around, and return to the kitchen, ignoring me completely. A crash of pots and pans would resound, followed by a stream of angry French.

Soon Lucienne would return, carrying a basket of bread. She would eye me with some slight amusement as if to say, "Well, this is the way families are—nothing to worry about." Sometimes I sat on the edge of my seat doggedly sipping my soup, expecting shots to ring out. None did, of course—at least for the time I was there. Lucienne sensed my concern, and with a twinkle in her eye set my mind at rest. She also did not hide her amusement at my brave but wretchedly spoken French and tried to help me although she knew no English.

In the last two days I stayed with this excitable family, business happily improved; the guests multiplied enough to fill half the tables of the restaurant. A few of them even took rooms. The father began to notice me, this time not unkindly, and once even winked at me. As usual, when the maximum number of guests were seated and eating, he proceeded to waltz out with his big beast of a dog. After performing with his dog a few minutes, he'd push the dog away and turn with great show to kissing and hugging and coo-cooing with his parakeet. This display of ferocious affection concluded, he gave a wild west yell and disappeared. The guests, who had waited patiently for him to complete his performance, sighed with relief and resumed eating. But Lucienne continued moving from guest to guest with her gracious, smiling self. She allowed neither the sudden boom in business, nor the lull in it, to affect her.

In time I was able to locate other quarters, hopeful that the atmosphere would be less hectic. The day before I left I impulsively gave Lucienne a religious medal and, of all things, a guide book on the Sanctuary. Actually the book was not intended for her, I bought it for myself because I thought it was written in English. Nevertheless she was delighted when I offered her the book. She immediately went off in a corner to read it.

The next day I saw her with the book in her hand. I brought down all my luggage and said good-bye to everybody: husband and wife, husband's brother, Pierre, and, of course, Lucienne. We shook hands and wished each other well. Lucienne accompanied me to the door and she thanked me. She said something else but I couldn't understand it. It didn't matter, for the look in her eyes said it. I started up the street, turned and waved at her. She stood by the door and waved back. Did I imagine I saw sadness in her eyes even though she was smiling? Never mind.

Lucienne—God love you, God love you all.

Lord, thank you for those of us who have the gift of courtesy, who make it easy for us to be good.

CHAPTER FIFTEEN

All Carry a Cross

July 30. Suffering is not limited to persons wearing plaster jackets or steel braces, persons hobbling on crutches or sitting in wheelchairs. The well and healthy spirit is not always contained by a body that stands observably erect; the invalid is not always the one whose position is observably prone.

Too many Christians—not only in Lourdes but elsewhere in the Christian world—hold the rather simplistic view that suffering is readily evident to the naked eye, that it is only physical infirmity that is worthy of compassion. Of course, I wouldn't want to exchange places with a person in a wheelchair. However, it is manifestly false to assume that because my neighbor does not sit in one or does not appear to be in visible distress, he is not suffering.

Indeed he may be suffering more than the man in the wheelchair. He may be schizophrenic or depressed. He may have lost a daughter, a son, a father, a mother. She may be a victim of rape, incest, alcoholism, poverty—all wounds that one does not see with the naked eye. There are any number of possibilities for suffering in people who do not show it. As Christians we are bound to anticipate suffering in our neighbor and to treat him or her with sensitivity and kindness.

Each of us carries a cross that is uniquely our own. Often we do not look at our neighbor closely enough to perceive this cross. We assume that as long as our neighbor looks well that he is not in need of anything. Looking at our neighbor in this way has had grievous consequences. It robs us—and them—of compassion.

If we examine the Gospel closely, we see that Christ did not die only for love of persons incapacitated or for persons on the verge of death. He does not intend that we love and serve only such persons. The lame and halt and blind of which the Gospels speak are visible signs of the plight and suffering of all of us, requiring an on-the-spot response.

Jesus repeatedly demonstrated this on-the-spot response. Love does not wait for visible targets; love assumes that all people everywhere and at all times are in need of our love.

My neighbor—which is to say my fellow-worker, brother, sister, friend, stranger—might conceivably be undergoing great anguish. He may not show it, or he may bring it to my attention. If he does give me a blow-by-blow description of his complaint, should I ridicule him for it? Should I condemn him to suffer silently because he has two arms and two legs, because he appears to be sound of body? Should I scorn him because he does not manifest the heroic forbearance of a saint? Should I refuse to hear him because he has asked me, in so many words, for that love that Paul defines as love which endures all, is patient, is kind, is not jealous, bears all things, believes all things, hopes all things, and rejoices in the truth (see 1 Corinthians 13:1-12)?

Too often we equate military heroism with heroic sanctity. Many Christians contend that to resent suffering is an act of rebellion against God, and that to be a true Christian the Christian should imitate Christ's total surrender to the cross. "My Father, if it is possible, take this cup of suffering from me! Yet not what I want, but what you want" (Mt 26:39).

In some mysterious way suffering is connected with our salvation, yes—but is it up to us to judge whether one man is deserving of our compassion, while another isn't? Are we required to add to his suffering simply because suffering is equated with salvation?

In the mystical revelations of Blessed Henry Suso written in A.D. 1327, he has God speaking to us with words that contradict the pleasure principle of our present-day world.

> Suffering converts a worldly person into a heavenly person. Suffering makes one a stranger to the world and gives him My continual intimacy. It decreases friends and increases grace. Suffering guards one against grave falls; it gives a person self-knowledge and makes him firm toward self and compassionate toward his neighbor... Suffering takes away sin, drives away temptations, quenches carnal desires and renews the spirit. Be convinced that it is a wholesome drink and the most beneficial herb of all paradise. It mortifies the body, which is destined to rot away, but nourishes the precious soul which is to endure eternally.[1]

Truly we are all called to surrender to the cross at the time that God requires us. But we should not make assumptions about our neighbor's cross, whether he carries it nobly or whether he complains as he carries it. We should see our neighbor as someone about whom we are forbidden to make any sort of judgment—as someone whose soul is responsible to God alone. We in our turn are responsible to God for what we do or fail to do. In the meantime if our neighbor should come to us for help, we should view him always as someone in need of our love no matter what his appearance may suggest.

We are called to love even those with whom we have little in common, or of whose lifestyle we may disapprove. In the days of

Jesus it was the person with leprosy, the disease of the sinner, the outcast. Such people were quarantined and placed in permanent ostracism, such as in the garbage-dump area of town, where everybody kept their distance from them and no doubt assumed that "such people" deserved what they got. Alas, there are those today who would do the same with people who have HIV or AIDS.

As Christians we are bound to acknowledge the mystery of suffering. Therefore, no one can presume to know what another person may or may not be enduring in his personal life. What we are bound to remember is that we are all imperfect human beings who need the help and encouragement of other imperfect human beings.

Lourdes, apart from being a place where pilgrims and pilgrim patients come to be cured of bodily infirmities, healed in soul, or strengthened in spirit, is primarily a place of worship. We go to Lourdes to receive from God the courage to love in order that we might practice that love. This love is needed most in the world in which we live; with persons with whom we live and work, with strangers we meet who may need a kind word, a sympathetic smile, a remembering of them to God in prayer.

But our love should also help us to seek to understand the times in which we live. "You can look at the earth and the sky and tell what it means; why, then, don't you know the meaning of this present time?" (Mt 16:3). In our day and age, Jesus would say, "You can go to the moon and split the atom; why, then, don't you know the meaning of this present time?" The meaning of the present time is to seek the peace that only Christ can give, for ourselves and for our neighbor—not the peace of military deterrence, which is maintained on the backs of the poor and needy of this world.

Of course, nothing is easier than to love in Lourdes; the thousands of pilgrim patients make it easy. It is much harder to bring this love into our everyday world and to put it to work. But if it is harder to love in the everyday world, it does not mean that the need to do so is less important, or requires less vigilance in how we see one other. If we kept in mind these words of Jesus, "love your neighbor as you love yourself" (Mt 19:19), the ripple effect of this love would change the world.

Lord, help us to reduce the number of
"spiritual casualties" in this world
by loving others as you first loved us.

CHAPTER SIXTEEN

Sister Marie's House of Love

August 1. In June when I arrived at Lourdes I went directly to L'Hospitalite de Notre Dame de Lourdes to sign in as a volunteer. I was told I could stay at L'Abri de St. Michel, a shelter house for volunteers situated in the Sanctuary itself. However, in order to stay there I had to have a letter of recommendation from a priest, which I didn't have. Although I wrote for one that same day, my letter of recommendation did not arrive from New York City until I was getting ready to leave Lourdes, two months later.

In the meantime I had to find my own accommodations. It wasn't hard; there were lots of them. I learned about Sister Marie's House of Love—which is what she called it—in the last month of my stay at Lourdes. When I heard that the house took in only English-speaking guests, I rushed to take it. I suppose my coming to stay with English-speaking people did little to improve my French, but it certainly made things easier for me.

Sister Marie Benigne, who ran the house, was a small, thin, fragile-looking woman. She hailed from Dublin, Ireland, and was cheerful, direct, and spontaneous. I liked her immediately. She was probably the world's worst businesswoman, which perhaps explains why her "house of love" wasn't a success, financially speaking. Her success had nothing to do with making money. She and her companion nun, Sister Marie Fidele, were successful, I believe, because they ran their house according to standards of Christian Love.

Sister Marie ran a guest house with all the amenities: the food was good and plentiful, the rooms adequately furnished and comfortable, the atmosphere friendly. Above all, the house had a spirit of goodwill that enveloped all who came to stay. There was a quiet, unpretentious piety among the guests, who came from countries all over the world: Ireland, England, Canada, the United States, Australia, Mauritania, French Morroco, and Dutch Guyana. When I asked Sister Marie to tell me what she charged for room and board, she said, "Give me what you can afford." I didn't know what to say to that. When she saw I didn't know what to do, she quoted an amount. I must say I agreed to it rather quickly. The price was right.

Sister Marie really did run a house of love. There were the four little French boys whom she took in from the Municipal Orphanage. She fed them, sheltered them, and sent them out on picnics with her young volunteer helpers for two weeks. It was not exactly good business, but it was very successful Christianity. When stranded pilgrims without a penny were fed and given lodging, that too was not good business, but it was Good Samaritan love. Another time she took in a group of old ladies from the Municipal Old Ladies Home, wining and dining them without charging them anything. God only knows what else she did in collaboration with her companion Sister Marie Fidele, but perhaps that is for the best. People such as Sister Marie Benigne and Sister Marie Fidele are at their best when they don't have nosey people monitoring their generosity.

I was particularly impressed with the young people helping her; they not only volunteered to do the cleaning, cooking, and shopping, they paid her for the food and lodging they received. I met many such young people at Lourdes; they were from all countries of the world and from all walks of life. I had the chance to talk with many of them; some of them were teenagers. I was touched by their concern for the afflicted of this world, for the hungry, the sick, the homeless, for the innocent victims of war; they wanted so much to help.

The young volunteers at Sister Marie's house spoke of missionary service to mankind; they were very serious about it. At the same time they laughed and joked and sang songs together and were so inspiriting they made everybody feel good. What I found touching and inspiring was these young people's love of Christ! By no means were they all headed for the convent and seminary, but they were all committed to Christ. They will be good teachers, doctors, sociologists, nurses, social workers, engineers, artists. I believe their faith will give their work a meaning and direction over and above those for whom work is simply a means of obtaining financial reward.

I should like to tell you about Anna and Steven, both Sister Marie helpers, and both in their late teens. They typified an attitude I found in many young persons I met at Lourdes. One night I came in late having worked the whole day at the train terminal. Because I often worked late, Sister Marie kindly gave me a key to the front door, which she locked every night at 12 o'clock.

When I came up the steps I noticed the light in the dining room was on. My heart leaped; it meant someone was having a late tea. Since it was a cold night, nothing would have served me better than to join whoever was having tea. I jumped the steps and threw open the door of the dining room. I closed the door immediately and went up to my room. What I saw in the dining room was truly touching. The English girl, Anna, and the Irish boy, Steven, were saying the Rosary together. The girl was kneeling before a statue of the Virgin Mary while the boy was seated to the right of her. "Holy Mary, Mother of God, pray for us sinners...."

I would have to wait to have my tea tomorrow. I didn't mind.

"Let us conduct ourselves properly, as people who live in the light of day..." (Rm 13:13). Lord, may we always strive to live in the light of day. Help us to follow the Christ within us so that we may always be in that light.

CHAPTER SEVENTEEN

Bernard

August 3. In appearance Bernard was unremarkable. Prematurely white-haired, he was about forty years old. He was of middle height, slightly rotund in figure. He was quick and strong, although he didn't look it. He liked to laugh and to make others laugh.

Once, during a work lull inside the volunteer shelter house barracks, the men started tossing things at each other in a playful way. Bernard joined in; he picked up a sock and threw it. Suddenly, three of the men at once took aim and threw various small objects at Bernard. As Bernard stood warding them off, a young fellow came up close and hit him on the temple with an apple—the smack was heard across the room.

Immediately the laughing and shouting stopped; the men watched Bernard to see what he would do. The young fellow who had thrown the apple stood there, laughing nervously. Bernard picked up the apple with a threatening show, but it was evident that he was going to keep it a joke. He threw the apple quite wide of the mark at the laughing young man.

Bernard brought this cheerfulness into his work with patients. He had his own way with them. Once I saw him lift an old woman, literally cradling her in his arms. As he carried her he looked directly into her eyes and, without taking his eyes from her, set her gently in a wheelchair. He always said something to the patient—"Bless you" or "In Christ's peace." He seemed to take a personal interest in his patients, and if there was time he talked to them.

Bernard treated his patients as if he had long made friends with them and that to help them was the most natural thing in the world. I watched patients smile at him as he lifted them or saw them turn round to him with gratefulness in their eyes as he wheeled them on ramp or platform. I think this is what made him different from the other volunteers: his personal touch. Bernard saw each patient not as freight to be moved from one place to another, but as a friend or next door neighbor that he had known for a long time.

Not all the volunteers at Lourdes handled the patients as Bernard did. I don't know that I did. I had to fight against a feeling of separation between myself and the patient; it was as if a person's illness somehow changed his human identity, as though he were no longer of this world. I struggled against the imaginary gulf between us—the gulf between the living and the departed. The patients themselves often brought me back to reality with a look or something they said, and made me see that there is no difference between us, that we are never departed from one another in this life or the next.

One day, at the crack of dawn, we gathered in the big station house behind Lourdes terminal to prepare ourselves for work. Every morning the first thing we did was pray the Lord's Prayer, then a Hail Mary, then a Glory Be. After a short litany of petitions covering every kind of need, we concluded with the words, *"St. Bernadette, priez pour nous"* (Pray for us). The chief of the volunteers then divided the men—about fifty of us—into teams or squads and assigned us to a particular platform. The day's schedule included hundreds of pilgrim patients arriving from all parts of Europe. I went with Bernard, who captained our team. We were a crack team of six Frenchmen and one American.

That day we worked car after car, transporting patients with every kind of malady, the sweat pouring down face, back, and chest until we were wringing wet. Bernard was everywhere at once, always with gentleness, patience, and a kind word. He never ordered us men around or told us what to do. There was no need. You just followed him, and did as he did. As I worked I could not help thinking that there are men who fight bloody wars, who take human lives and all too often give their lives, in sacrifice, often for the worst possible reasons.

Here in Lourdes, the commitment is to works of mercy and the spending of self for love of God. How nice if all the world could be slaves to love instead of slaves to violence and war. I breathed a prayer of thanks to the Blessed Mother for making this grace-filled oasis of mercy possible, for putting us all to work in service to God's love.

At the end of the day, after hundreds of patients had safely passed through our hands, we stood in the big station house, all of us looking half-dead. Bernard stood with his sweaty shirt plastered to his back. He looked dazed, as if the last drop of blood had been wrung from him. I am not normally a demonstrative man, but when I saw Bernard standing there on the platform like a man in shock, I couldn't help myself. I went to him, grabbed his hand and started pumping it. He looked surprised. Quickly he caught himself and started smiling.

A man is known by the way he treats a stranger. If he is kind to someone whom he will probably never see again, he pleases Christ—Christ who told the tale of the kindness of the Good Samaritan. What I'm trying to say is that although I spoke little French, and Bernard even less English, yet I believe that through

Christ we understood each other. Bernard and I spoke to each other through Christ's love which I believe is the one language common to all mankind.

The day before Bernard left Lourdes to return to his home in Brittany, we sat over a cup of *café au lait*. I was trying to tell him how angry I was with myself for not taking greater pains to learn French. For I believed this glaring omission was cutting into my Lourdes experience, diminishing it despite the wonderful things I was experiencing. Once he understood what I was saying, Bernard immediately took out pad and pencil and began to teach me. Why compound omission with delay? For the next two hours we sat sipping *café au lait* and pronouncing French words.

Bernard was about forty years old, married, and the father of three children. I didn't learn much more than that about him. Neither did I ask him what sort of work he did. For I knew that whatever work he did for a living, he did it for love of God, and his neighbor was bound to benefit.

What struck me about this Frenchman from Brittany was this: Bernard saw Christ in everybody. After all, the practice of the Christian religion is, plain and simple, the practice of love. Jesus was the consummate practitioner of this love. The whole point of life is to follow Christ. Everything else we do is beside the point. For example, if there were no miracle stories in the Gospels, the Gospel message would remain essentially intact. That message is clear and unequivocal: First, God is love. Second, we are to love as God loves (if we are ever to be with God). I believe Bernard in his own way beautifully demonstrated this love.

Lord, help us to follow you—
each in our own way. Amen.

CHAPTER EIGHTEEN

God's Children of Light

August 11. The two buses pulled into the station, each carrying about sixty spastic children from Belgium. The children had been driven from the Shrine to the Lourdes train terminal, and now were on their way home again. They looked sleepy-eyed, as though they might have been taken too quickly from their hospice beds. The early morning darkness kept everybody in shadows. Both men and children seemed subdued.

Not even the harsh glare of the Kleig lights in the big terminal house did much to dispel the gloom. Darkness or not, the work of getting the children into wheelchairs and down the gangplank from bus to platform, then lifting them and carrying them bodily into the trains, had begun.

These children were on one of many organized pilgrimages to visit Lourdes during the seasonal months (from March to October). As accorded each pilgrimage, the children were allowed one week to participate in the traditional ceremonies, to occupy a bed at the hospice, and to receive care. At the end of that they had to leave, to make room for the next contingent of sick pilgrims. This was standard procedure: It ensured that all the sick who were visiting Lourdes would be given the same opportunity to receive healing.

I discovered that these particular children had come to Lourdes accompanied only by nurses and doctors. No parents. This surprised me: Spastic children are not easy to care for. It occurred to me that the parents of these children must have had great faith to entrust their children to the care and volunteer work of strangers.

As for me, I was not so secure in my faith. If we presuppose a divine order where everything is supposed to harmonize, where everyone performs his task according to his ability and knowledge and opportunity, where precisely did these afflicted children fit into the scheme? What was the point of their suffering and help-lessness? Were they created simply to be a burden to their parents? Or to be reminders to the rest of us that we should regard ourselves as more fortunate?

The truth is, I didn't see any purposeful place for them in the world at first. At best I saw these children as a challenge to the exercise of everyone's charity—from their parents to strangers like myself.

It was still dark when we began moving the children from the buses to the trains, and a full moon was up. For some reason, the lights in the departing trains hadn't been turned on. Neither were the platform lights, which meant we had to work the platforms in semi-darkness. Inside the trains, all was dark. As we entered the cars, holding on to our little patients, we had to feel our way, step by step, through the narrow passageway. It was hot and cramped in those cars. My back and hands were wet with perspiration, and the little girl I carried almost slipped from my grasp. I held on to her with growing panic, afraid that I'd drop her before we reached the assigned compartment of the train. When at last I reached compartment number six I found two children—a little boy and girl—already installed in it. I placed the little girl beside the other two; all three now lay on a mattress that had been placed across the seats of the compartment. I looked down at them in the half-shadows, relieved that the little girl was safely installed. I guessed their ages were between three and five years old.

I stood a moment, looking at them in the semi-darkness. Suddenly moonlight passing through the car window fell on them, bathing them in a queer, ghostly light. What I saw astonished me: illuminated by the moonlight, all three children lay with their faces incandescent with joy, each one smiling into the embrace of something that reflected in their faces, giving each child an expression of unearthly beauty. It seemed a hunter's moon had come searching and cornered God's loveliest quarry. Each child gazed with angelic happiness into this other shining world—a gaze that took me in it, searching me with a light that felt like fire, evoking in me a sense of things beyond this world.

I returned to the platform to pick up the next child, and the next, astonished to see on each face the same joy, the same gladness of spirit, the same shining reflection of something "wonderfully other" in their expressions.

To this day I think about those smiling faces with wonder. Perhaps what I saw in their faces is the other life, the wonder and joy and rightness of this life for which St. Paul says "all of creation groans with pain... as we wait for God to make us his sons and daughters and set our whole being free" (Rom 8:22-23).

From that moment on, however, I understood the place of these children, understood what was uniquely theirs to give: one more side of God's love, revealed through the unique beings of these helpless children!

The volunteer men, some of them pretty rough fellows, wept at the sight of these poor, uncoordinated, quivering little bodies. I think I understood what they were feeling: the mystery of suffering and of God's love for us that radiated through these children. "How fortunate you are," Jesus tells his disciples in Luke 10:23, "to see the things you see! I tell you many prophets and kings wanted to see what you see, but they could not, and to hear what you hear, but they did not." We were fortunate indeed to see God's children of light that August morning!

If I was looking to justify the existence of these helpless, sick children, I was given my answer. For what greater thing than to be a lightning rod for God's grace? We may lament for these children, that they are afflicted and suffer, yet who among us can give to fellow human beings the blinding sense of life with which these children filled us?

10:00 A.M. The children are safely aboard the train. The work is done. The men stand looking after the departing train. They are silent. The moon, which had lighted the town of Lourdes with its ghostly light till the wee hours, has vanished. Now the sun shines. The light bathing the green hills, the light spinning through the delicate morning haze, laying gleaming shafts of light across the tracks. The train's rattling sounds grow smaller and smaller; the back of the train turns a curve, vanishes.

Suddenly these children of light and that whole midsummer August morning in the little town of Lourdes, are God's....

> *Lord, in your eyes, there is no such thing as*
> *"senseless" suffering. May our trials*
> *here transform us more completely*
> *into the iamge of you Son.*

CHAPTER NINETEEN

Grotto Roundtable

August 12, 11:00 P.M. "'Penance, penance, penance.' When I hear those words I think of a spanking," said Philip. The others laughed. Philip loved to play devil's advocate. He was a seminary student in Valladolid, Spain.

We were seated on a slab of rock situated on the other side of the Gave de Pau River (usually it was simply called "the Gave"), facing the Grotto of the Apparitions. There were Anna from England, age 18, and Darina from Ireland, age 26, both volunteer nurse's aids. The *brancardiers* were Philip from England, age 23; Vincent from Scotland, age 30; and Erik from Canada, age 17.

Since we were all English-speaking we sometimes gathered at Sister Marie's House of Love at the end of a long day, mostly for prayer, but sometimes for what turned out to be roundtable discussions on religion. We talked about women's ordination, married priests, birth control, abortion, papal infallibility. The talks were unplanned, spontaneous. Anna was the one who brought up the subject of Our Lady's messages to Bernadette.

"You're making light of it, Philip. It doesn't mean that at all," said Anna, smiling.

"Well, what do the words mean?" said Philip. "Don't we get

enough penance in this life? We're smothered in it."

"You're equating penance with pain. It isn't." said Vincent.

"How can you say pain is not involved in acts of penance?" said Philip, shrugging his shoulders.

"You're thinking of penance in terms of fasting, wearing a hair-shirt, flagellation, that sort of thing," answered Vincent. "For some people, the practice of austerities can bring them to love of God and neighbor. For the rest of us, I think, it is hard enough to do God's will each day. All meaningful penance is intended to help one to grow in charity."

"Yes, I think so," said Anna. "Penance is not punishment, penance is correction."

"Exactly," said Erik. "And to correct myself means to practice Christ's teachings."

"Any kind of learning requires effort and every honest effort takes in pain," said Vincent, an ex-seminary student who taught school in Glasgow. "Oh no—we cannot escape pain in this life."

"I would like to see us try. We're so put together we can't escape it. You're right there," said Philip with a trace of annoyance.

"Penance, penance, penance," repeated Vincent. "Three words which could change the world. The Virgin Mary knew very well what she was saying. Imagine if we did the penance required to help us see things with the eyes of Christ. Why, we would see reality as Christ saw it in his day without distortions or illusions!"

"So many things would change. For one thing, if we saw the world with the love of Christ we would stop being so nationalistic," Darina said.

"Are you suggesting turning against our own country..." said Philip with a mischievous gleam in his eye.

"Not at all," put in Darina, "I mean we would stop placing so much importance on nationality. I'm thinking of the Irish problem of centuries and all the violence that it has engendered and I'm sick of it. Imagine Christ, whose meat was to do the will of the Father, joining the nationals or patriots of his time..."

"Zealots—they were called zealots!" interposed Erik.

"Yes," Darina went on, "Christ leading his countrymen against the hated Romans who occupied their country. I can't imagine it."

"I think you're quite right," I said. "Nothing in the Gospels suggests that Christ was the slightest bit concerned with the territorial integrity of his country. As for the society in which he lived, he was scarcely in agreement with it."

"I agree with Vincent," Anna said. "Penance means conforming our lives to the will of God..."

"Pray tell me, what is that will?" said Philip. "I am always hearing about that will, like a snowplow. Get out of my way—here comes my will!" His eyes twinkled with amusement.

"It's unfortunate the word 'will' is used in the language like a battering ram. God's will is the law of life," Vincent responded.

"God's will commands us to love one another," Anna said.

"And why should he have to command us?"

"Because," laughed Anna, "we're willful, we're selfish, and because we ask silly questions."

"You hit the nail on the head. We ask too many questions," said young Erik.

"Oh, I don't think we ask enough questions. That's why nobody understands anybody, and we never know what the other is saying," replied Philip in a very serious tone of voice. "We're meek when we should be aggressive, and we're aggressive all in the wrong ways."

"I get your point," Vincent said. "But now let's stick to Our Lady's messages. The eighteen visitations of the Virgin Mary to

St. Bernadette, beginning February 11, 1858 and ending July 16, 1858, have a significance far beyond the human situation of that time."

Philip snorted. "You don't say. What significance? We still live in a barbarous world. Indeed, genocide is becoming a routine practice of war, and few people are raising their voices in outrage against it. It's ironical that the practitioners of this new device for killing happen to be Christians who have been taught by their Church that killing fellow human beings is wrong."

We looked for that twinkle in Philip's eye; it wasn't there.

Vincent cleared his throat. "Those who do these things are not Christians. Jesus spoke about wolves in sheep's clothing."

Philip laughed. "Well, I wish we could unmask these wolves of their sheep's clothing. We seem to pay more heed to the voice of wolves than to the voice of Christ."

"Philip, I know what you're getting at. But another time. How I look at it, if we're still on the subject of Our Lady's messages—I mean the point of the visitations was to demonstrate God's concern for us; through Bernadette, Our Lady offers crucial insights toward the spiritual deliverance of the entire human race."

"Tall order," said Philip. "But we already have the crucial insights through Christ, we have the means of deliverance through Christ. How many times do we have to be provided with the means?"

"As often as it takes," answered Vincent. "Our Lady simply paraphrases her son. Take the words, 'Pray for sinners.' What do they make you think of?"

"I can't imagine," said Philip.

"Do you remember the story Christ tells about the publican and Pharisee?"

"Yes."

"'Pray for sinners.' Ah, who are the sinners?"

"Why, we are, of course," said Darina.

"That's what I'm getting at," said Vincent, blowing through his cheeks. "Let us be careful that our praying is not like the Pharisee of the Gospels, who preened himself on how good he was."

"Exactly," affirmed Darina. "We should be careful how we see ourselves and how we see those for whom we pray—especially those who happen to be unlike us."

Vincent leaned forward as if to emphasize what he would say. "Good point. When Our Lady therefore tells us to 'pray for sinners,' I must, if my praying is honest, begin with myself. After all, who is the sinner with whom I am most familiar? Why, myself. And who is the sinner about whom I know least, even as I am tempted to believe that I know so much? Why, my neighbor. Do not suppose that because I do not sin mortally—and a lot of us have a somewhat legalistic notion of what sinning unto death is—that I am right with God."

Vincent continued, enunciating clearly in his Scottish brogue. "What will God ask us on the day of our judgment? Will he ask how often we attended church service? How often we pray? How well we obey the laws of man? How well and faithfully we pay our taxes? How well we serve and defend our country against its enemies? How well we die for our country? How well we hate the enemies of religion and seek their destruction? I do not think so. God will ask us one question and our salvation will depend on what our answer is. That question is: How much have we loved?"

"You should be the priest, Vincent," said Philip, "not me."

"Oh don't say that. We need you," Anna said.

"How about this one?" said Erik, reading out of a Lourdes guide book. "'Go and drink at the spring and wash in it.'"

"You tell me," said Philip.

"I don't want to do all the talking," said Vincent.

"All right. Imagine Bernadette gathering a mixture of earth and water in the hollow of her hand and drinking and washing herself with it," said Anna.

"Symbolically the muddy water," said Erik, "is ourselves before we have been spiritually purged..."

"Yes, it has to do with conversion," Anna said.

"Water is symbol for a lot of things," Darina said.

Philip laughed. "Water is the symbol of the life of God received at baptism. Check to see if I'm right. I learned that, of course, at seminary."

"I learned it in Sunday school," said Erik.

"It is getting the log out of our eye so we can see ourselves and each other," said Darina. "That is the beginning of conversion."

"There's another way to see it," I said. "Conversion is hearing in ourselves the 'small voice' of God, that is, if we are not being smothered to death by endless distractions. If it is the voice of God we hear, it shall be the voice of love."

"You see," said Vincent, "nothing Our Lady says is not in some way a paraphrase of her Son."

Anna said, "'You will kiss the earth for sinners.' How do you connect that with the Gospels?"

"More symbols," answered Darina. "On one level the earth is a sign of our mortality, the dust from which we derive and the dust to which we will return. On another level, it is God's sign of the gift of life to us."

"It is through the dust of the earth that we receive our daily bread," put in Erik.

"We kiss the earth in thanksgiving to God for the abundance of the earth's lifegiving resources," said Darina.

"Yes, but what do these words signify: 'You will kiss the earth for sinners'—beside appearing to be an act of homage and supplication?" said Philip.

"Kiss the earth," I said, "signifies kissing on behalf of those sinners among us who are destroying it. We are destroying it by means of pollution and exploitation as surely as if we were doing it with thermonuclear intercontinental missiles or B-29 saturation bombing."

"Oh, I don't know if I agree with that," said Philip. "Genesis has God say clearly to Adam and Eve, 'Be fruitful, multiply, fill the earth and conquer it.'"

"Conquer doesn't mean destroy," said Darina. "Kiss the earth for sinners means, to repent that we are party, even indirectly, to destroying the earth. For God made the earth for us to build on, not to destroy."

"I know what you're going to say, Darina. We are on this earth in order that, little by little, we learn how to love one another in rehearsal for the heavenly life. Is that it?" said Philip.

Smiling, Darina nodded.

Philip went on. "We practice our love skills here in order some day to bring these skills with us to practice in heaven. Is that it?"

Darina said simply, "Yes."

"Well, I agree," said Philip, the devil's advocate. And we all laughed.

Lord, help us never to deviate from your
will. Above all, help us to understand
that your will is our life.

CHAPTER TWENTY

Erik

August 16. Erik prayed as easily as some people tell stories. This Canadian boy from Ottawa was unusually mature for a seventeen-year-old; his gift of prayer made him special. He prayed aloud and he prayed to himself. He prayed at Mass and he prayed with friends. The first day I met him he initiated our friendship by suggesting that we "say the Rosary together."

So we crossed the bridge to the other side of the Gave to the beautiful meadow opposite the Grotto, and walked back and forth, saying the Rosary. He finished each decade with a prayer of petition, for members of his family, for friends, and, not infrequently, for strangers. Or he would examine his conscience aloud and say, "You know, I'm not seeing this in the light of Christ's charity."

Erik came on us like a fresh mountain breeze. He made friends easily and, since he spoke French tolerably well, he moved with freedom not only among the volunteers but among sick pilgrims as well. I saw him reach out to people in his warm and joyful way. I frequently saw him exchanging his name and address with those he met.

Erik threw himself into work enthusiastically, without thought of spending himself. He worked at the Lourdes railroad station carrying and wheeling patients, on the autobus taking patients to and from the Sanctuary, and at the airport taking patients off the plane (a sometimes ticklish undertaking) and onto the bus for transportation to the Sanctuary. He worked in the *piscines* (baths), handling patients who are anything but pleasing to look at and touch, and always with zest and energy and caring good-will. When he wasn't working, he went to Mass or participated in the afternoon Procession of the Blessed Sacrament. He especially liked to take part in the hauntingly lovely *Procession aux Flambeaux* (Procession of Fire) in the cool of the evening.

Many a starlit night we got together to pray and to discuss spiritual things. Erik's spontaneity was contagious; he was an example to the men and women who gathered with him, some of whom were very young. He helped us to speak out, and some of us contributed spiritual insights worth remembering. His maturity of spirit reminded me of St. Paul's words to Timothy: "Do not let anyone look down on you because you are young, but be an example for the believers in your speech, your conduct, your love, faith, and purity" (1 Tm 4:12).

On the day before leaving Lourdes to return to his home in Canada, Erik and I, having finished a work stint at the train station, walked through thick crowds during the noon hour on our way to the tiny bridge which spanned the Gave. We intended to cross the bridge and relax in a lovely wooded spot set by the rushing waters of the river. When we got there Erik suggested that we say the Rosary, and I agreed. We looked for a spot to sit, but the benches were taken by pilgrims.

Suddenly Erik darted down to the edge of the river, straight to a slab of rock that jutted out into the water, and sat on it. I came down after him quickly, and there we sat. And so, back to back, we began saying the Glorious Mysteries of the Rosary—while children played around us, and pilgrims sat nearby eating their lunch. We continued praying by the flowing waters, with the noon-day sun shining, until we completed the Hail Holy Queen.

Erik was one whose youth did not deter him from making friends with his God, from talking to him as to one who listens and understands. May we, like Erik, learn to listen and understand the counsels of God throughout our lives.

> *Oh Lord, in the words of the psalmist,*
> *"You are my defender and protector.*
> *You are my God; in you I trust" (Ps 91:2).*

CHAPTER TWENTY-ONE

The Seeker

August 17. I was coming out of the Place de Tilleuls, a tree-shaded park near the Palais du Justice, when a young man came up to me and asked, "Do you speak English?"

"Yes," I replied, wondering what he wanted. He fell in step with me as we walked in the brilliant noonday sun down the Avenue du Foch. "Do you by chance know where the Grotto is?" he asked. His accent sounded English to me, although he later informed me he was Australian.

"By chance," I said, "I am on my way there now."

"Ah, I'm in luck," he smiled, and added, "Mind if I come along?"

We chatted the whole way. His name was Mack, and he was a school teacher. He had rented a car in London and had already traveled with it up and down Europe. He had just come in from Spain, and was on his way to the soccer games in Germany.

I was curious to know what made him want to visit Lourdes. His mother, he explained, had recently become a Catholic and had spoken of Lourdes. The things he heard her say about Lourdes fascinated him, especially the story about water coming up out of the ground where none had been before.

He was referring to the miraculous spring appearing the day

after the Ninth Apparition of the Virgin Mary to Bernadette. He wondered, he said, whether these things were true and were not embellished superstitions. We walked and talked, and though he put questions to me I didn't think he expected that I give him answers, or even that I had answers to give him. They were questions on those mysteries that we all ponder from time to time: Do ghosts exist? Has anyone really come back from the dead? Are the miracle stories in the Gospels true?

We pushed our way through thick crowds on Rue de la Grotte, the long winding street which led to the Sanctuary. The atmosphere of Lourdes outside the Sanctuary—it has 500 hotels in a town of 30,000—had the look of a perpetual bazaar. I wondered what Mack thought of the rows of shops selling religious articles of every description (there were hundreds of such shops), of the great drone of human voices chattering away in foreign tongues. But Mack didn't say anything.

To some visiting pilgrims and tourists, the buying and selling of knick-knacks and religious articles is offensive, unspiritual, mercenary, and so forth. And yet, merchant houses were numerous even in the days of Christ. The Holy One himself walked in our midst and endured unspiritual vulgarity. It did not stop him from proclaiming God's love, nor keep him from loving us. Why should it stop us from loving one another?

"I almost didn't make it here, you know." Mack had been unable to get a room for the night near the French-Spanish border and had driven the whole night. If he had gotten that room he would probably have bypassed Lourdes and gone to the next town. "I intend to stay for only a few hours," he said. "My next stop is Munich. After that I'll have to get rid of the car—my insurance runs out at the end of this month."

Our conversation passed to other subjects, and Mack brought up again his mother's conversion to Roman Catholicism. In almost the same breath he brought up a man named Jack, an

Irishman and long-time friend of the family. His mother's conversion was due in no small way to this man, for Jack had been able to explain his Catholic faith with prodigious knowledge and eloquent flair. Mack was obviously impressed by this. Jack had looked into other religions, Mack explained, but other religions failed to provide him with answers that satisfied him.

Although he did not say so directly, Mack seemed to be a little jealous of his mother's faith, as though she had received a great gift.

"Are you thinking of becoming a Catholic?" I asked.

He didn't answer my question directly. "I was brought up an Episcopalian."

Mack looked awed as we entered the Sanctuary. We came in through the Bernadette Soubirous entrance and made our way across Rosary Square toward the Grotto. The superimposed Basilicas, the statue of the Crowned Virgin, the Esplanade des Processions, are truly impressive sights. I was hoping I could persuade him to take part in the Torchlight Procession that evening.

At last we stood at the opening of the Grotto. At its center is an altar. Above the altar, only a little behind it, hangs a string of discarded crutches, steel braces, and the like. On the right side of the altar is a deep recess in the rock, about twenty-five feet high, in which the Virgin Mary is said to have stood. A statue of the Virgin Mary stands in its place.

Mack and I got behind other pilgrims in line to pass into the interior of the Grotto. Once inside we paused to pray. Then, as was the custom, we kissed the hallowed rock of the Grotto as it had been kissed by millions and millions of pilgrims before us. We passed between the altar and the standing arrangement of lighted candles, with the Soul's Letter Box placed next to it; pilgrims dropped in this letterbox their petitions.

I brought Mack to the water taps and tried to explain what I didn't fully understand myself. On February 25, 1858, the Virgin commanded Bernadette to "go and drink at the spring and wash in it." Bernadette looked for the spring, but there was no spring in sight, only the rushing water of the Gave about a hundred feet away. She headed in the direction of the river; then hesitated, turning her steps back to the grotto. Again she halted and looked as though to question the "lady." Then she dropped to her knees and dug up with her hands a little of the earth, thus forming a hollow which soon filled with muddy water. Bernadette was seen to raise this water to her lips, to drink it and to wash her face with it. On her return to the rock in front of the grotto entrance, where she went into ecstasy again, her face was smeared with mud.

Meanwhile those assembled at the grotto were mystified. They were disappointed. To many of them, it appeared that Bernadette was no longer responsible for her actions. "The poor child has become insane," they cried. They turned away and went home.

The hollow in the earth that Bernadette had scooped out with her hands, however, continued to increase. That evening a trickle of water was slowly making its way towards the Gave. On the following morning there was a considerable flow. Today, the spring pointed out by the Virgin Mary continues to flow at a rate of 20,000 gallons each day.

Mack listened and then said, "Astonishing! It's rather hard to believe. Isn't it possible the spring was there underground the whole time?"

"Not according to a study made," I said. "Skeptics existed in those days too, and they made sure to investigate it. Besides, the circumstances of water appearing in the dramatic way it did at command of the Virgin Mary doesn't leave much to chance, does it?"

"It's an astonishing story," Mack agreed.

❧

Later Mack and I went to a coffee house on Place Jeanne D'Arc, and chatted about the mysterious thing called faith. He asked me what I meant by "faith."

"Faith," I said, trying to remember my own experience, "is God awakening in us his presence—generally at a critical time in our life. In this awakening, which can be abrupt or gradual, we become aware that we are embarked on a journey (sometimes by a circuitous route) to life, to God. It is God who provides us with our means of travel—our means of travel to God is by way of God's love. Does that make sense? The journey to God, even with God's help, is fraught with radical, sometimes painful, ordeals."

"Where does the Church fit into this?" Mack asked.

"First the Church helps to bring out this faith in us, helps to define it, helps to order it, to prune it in ourselves, so that it will bear good fruit. Second, the Church helps us through sacramental means to bear the ordeals."

Abruptly I stopped. I looked at Mack. He sat with eyes looking straight ahead. Nevertheless I felt I had said enough.

"What you say is interesting," Mack said, "but, you know, I'm not really thinking of becoming a Catholic." He added, smiling, "I'm just looking into it."

After a while I said, "Look, if you'd like to stay overnight, I can take you to Sister Marie's guest house. You'll feel at home there—they are all English-speaking."

In the evening we went to the Candlelight Procession. No one who visits Lourdes, for whatever reason, should miss this ceremony; it is primarily for laypeople and is hauntingly lovely. It takes place each evening at 8:30, beginning with the public recitation of the Rosary at the Grotto. The pilgrims begin the procession holding lighted candles, each joining in the singing of the Lourdes hymn, the "Ave Maria."

Slowly the pilgrims move in procession round the Esplanade and back to the Basilica until the sixty verses of the Abbe Gaignet's processional hymn have been sung. Between the singing and the lighted candles and the stars above, we are led imperceptibly into a dreamy meditation on the mysteries of this life. The words of the psalmist come to mind.

O Lord, our Lord, your greatness is seen in all the world! Your praise reaches up to the heavens; it is sung by children and babies.... When I look at the sky, which you have made, at the moon and the stars, which you set in their places— what is man, that you think of him; mere man, that you care for him?   PSALMS 8:1-4

After the Procession, we walked back to Sister Marie's house. Mack planned to leave the next day. I suggested he attend the 11:15 Pilgrim's Day Mass. He seemed willing. Since I had to be at work at the Lourdes train station at 5 o'clock in the morning, I wasn't sure whether I could make it with him. I suggested he ask someone at Sister Marie's to take him.

That night I thought about Mack, whether I had answered his questions. I felt sure that God had drawn him to Lourdes, and I felt sure that God was answering his mother's prayers. I was not so sure where I fit in, if at all.

The next day, as I lay across a bench, exhausted, waiting for the next trainload of patients, I heard my name called out. It was Mack. He had attended the Pilgrim's Day Mass and had come to say good-bye to me. At this moment a busload of patients arrived from the Sanctuary for departure. About nine patients were lined up one after the other to be wheeled to the waiting train.

I looked at Mack and then I looked at the patients lined up, and all in a flash I prayed, Lord, if Mack could only experience what I have experienced working with your pilgrim patients; you might tell him what he wants to know about faith, so that what I was not able to do yesterday with all my words, you, in a twinkling, will do.

"Mack," I said, "before you leave, would you help us wheel a patient to the train?"

"Yes," he said. He came back a few minutes later, having delivered his patient. "I see what you mean," he said, smiling.

When I saw Mack returning with the empty wheelchair—his face all lit up in a smile—I knew that God had touched him. God had touched me during my stay at Lourdes, again and again. "I tell you," Jesus says, "whenever you did this for one of the least important of these brothers of mine, you did it for me!" (Mt 25:40). Truly it is Christ in the soul of the patient who thanks you. How else can one explain the quickening in the heart I felt, the joy, the sense of the rightness of what I was doing, above all, the singing gratefulness I felt toward God for the privilege of serving my brothers and sisters!

We shook hands. He said, "Thanks. Maybe we'll meet again some time." As he said this, one of the men of my team grabbed my arm, notifying me a UNITALSI train from Caglieri was just then rolling in on track six. I had to go. As I started away I called after Mack, "Good luck." Mack waved and was gone.

Lord, we may never know until we get to heaven how much we have touched the lives of others. But help us to never stop reaching out.

CHAPTER TWENTY-TWO

The Town Crier

August 20. In our day and age, town criers have been supplanted by highpowered newscasts hourly transmitting the catastrophes of the world on radio and television. Lourdes is not without its hourly newscasts, but Lourdes, in keeping with its ancient days, also has a town crier.

This town crier makes his public announcements the old-fashioned way, proclaiming them through the streets of the town. His guttural cry can be heard loud and clear—not at night when everybody is preparing to retire, but in the light of day when everybody is up and running around.

You might want to know who this town crier was. Why, a dog. And you might wonder, *How could a dog become town crier? Did he run for office? Was he appointed?* I don't think any Lourdes official appointed him, nor do I think he ran for office. I think he gave himself the job. For this was no ordinary dog. This was a dog with a conscience, a dog with a noble cast of spirit.

I saw this dog charge straight into a traffic jam on the corner of Rue de la Grotte and Place du Marcadal, barking up a storm. He was less than middle size, with a white fur coat bright with red speckles. Besides the barking, there was a look on this dog's face of desperate rage—eyes bulging apoplectically—as if to say,

"How dare you? How dare you clutter up my street!"

My town crier hurled his message at buses, autos, motorcycles, and trucks that stood in caravan formation, waiting for the traffic light to change. "How dare you stand there leaking your filthy gas fumes and polluting my air! How dare you spread toxic contaminations in these beautiful Pyrenees!"

Indeed, "How Dare You" was a fitting title for the noble beast. The animal never ceased barking and lunging at these carbon-monoxide-producing vehicles; neither did the size of the passing vehicle intimidate him. On the contrary, How Dare You kept up his attack until these vehicles, both large and small, sputtered on out of town.

At first I didn't know what my town crier expected to achieve through his rather disorganized and solitary protests. To begin with, no one paid attention to him—or about as much attention as people pay to concerned environmentalists in my own country. But like any committed activist, How Dare You wasn't counting the cost. It was as though he believed that if you keep at something you really believe in, and believe what you are doing is for the common good, you'll eventually get people's attention, though not always are you going to generate a fitting response nor are you going to be thanked for it. In this day and age, where the common good threatens the uncommon few who have the power, you might even get into trouble for it.

Anyway, as I was coming up with a friend off Rue de la Grotte late one afternoon, I heard such a commotion I thought it was a riot taking place. It turned out to be How Dare You: His barking and rushing at the wheels of automobiles had literally stopped traffic. We saw him rush at the bumper and wheels of a big mack truck. Close your eyes and imagine this mammoth truck held at bay by my little pipsqueak of a dog!

I came upon this dog many times during the two months of my stay in Lourdes. When he wasn't combating trucks and automobiles, he looked neither ferocious nor apoplectic but rather meditative. Several times I saw him come down on Rue du Bourg street headed toward Rue du Fort, a short distance from Musee Pyreneen and the Chateau Fort. I suspect he lived in the immediate area. In fact, the street on which I saw How Dare You was just around the corner from Cachot de Bernadette, the little house St. Bernadette occupied with her family during the Apparitions. Indeed I could not help feeling there was a connection between my dog and Bernadette, who sees from heaven all our unheeding, bungling ways.

At any rate, every time I saw How Dare You pass down this street, with his head bowed, he gave every sign of being deep in thought. It was hard for me to believe this was the dog of ferocious bark and reckless lunge. However, I recognized the dog's white fur coat, bright with red speckles.

I was astounded by the expression on his face. He rather looked like the knight of the woeful countenance, his noble green eyes not protruding the slightest bit! This dog turned to me, his eyes so expressive that if he had said anything to me, such as, "Monsieur, have you a moment?" I would not have been surprised. For I saw in the eyes of this dog a thoughtful concern that I do not often see in human beings. I suppose I have grown accustomed to those of us who too often carry a look of apathy— the look of being swallowed up by everyday cares. Looking at this dog, however, I could not help thinking, "What wonderful spirit in those eyes. How could this creature be only a dog?" I wonder whether it was this spirit that St. Francis saw in animals—and loved them for it?

Awhile later, however, when my dog passed onto Rue de la Grotte where all the streaming traffic lay, no creature underwent a quicker transformation. Gone was the softly meditative gaze! My dog became animated, taut, watchful: Immediately the apoplectic "how-dare-you" look came into his face. He was preparing himself to act, and he did. He rushed at a smelly garbage truck with a machine gun-like bark.

Another time I saw my activist town crier chasing himself round and round in a circle; he was doing this in full view of everybody. What was the meaning of it? Who knows. Perhaps he was describing some of us. A few minutes later I saw this same dog trot along on Rue du Fort, quite silent again, with those same intensely grieving eyes. But why so?

Well, if you consider my dog's criticism, symbolically conveyed and communicated with often baleful directness, you might agree that he was surely on the side of the angels. For example, you don't have to be an activist to condemn, as my dog did with a piercing bark, a boy racing his motorcycle straight up Rue de la Grotte doing at least eighty miles an hour. Since it was still daylight the crowds on the street just about had time to get out of the lunatic's way.

This should give one an idea how things stood with How Dare You. The question begs asking: What was there about the town of Lourdes that motivated How Dare You to do combat on its behalf?

To begin with, Lourdes is a town with all the amenities of a city: It has a church, a square of tree-shade with a World War I monument and benches; a shoe shop, chemist shop, barber shop, and other shops. People live in houses requiring maintenance; they have to eat and clothe themselves and, like everybody else, are required to work in order to live. Hence, despite St. Bernadette's Apparitions and the millions of pilgrims annually visiting Lourdes along with all the extraordinary happenings for which Lourdes is known, life goes on. Which means Lourdes has its quota of obnoxious persons—I met a few of them. On the other hand, I happened also to meet many warm-hearted, friendly, helpful Lourdes townspeople who went out of their way to help us pilgrims and tourists, asking nothing in return.

My point is that my activist town crier would not waste his breath on something he didn't love. His daily lunging and wrathful barking at cars, which he did in order to protest those things he thought harmful, not to say dangerous, were done for love of the people of Lourdes.

One day, as I was seated at one of the sidewalk cafes on Rue Lafitte, enjoying a *cafe espress* and munching on a piece of croissant, my How Dare You came frothing down the street. I could not help noticing his face, especially the eyes and nostrils, which were absolutely quivering with emotion. What could be the matter? I thought.

The dog went right by me in a steady lope down the street. I stood up to get a better look at him for, as you might have surmised, I had grown fond of the little critter. He was probably the most conscientious and civic-minded dog I have ever known, more conscientious and civic-minded than a lot of people I know.

I watched my dog head out on Avenue Francis, which leads directly out of town in the direction of the Pic du Jer. How Dare You soon disappeared down the long street.

I sat down, lit my pipe, and pondered my friend's path. This was unlike him. What did he mean by going off like this? Did he know the mess he was leaving behind? Why, automobiles hooting madly, motorcycles, scooters, jeeps roaring back and forth, trucks rumbling, buses croaking; their collective exhausts were pouring out blankets of carbon monoxide fumes. The air stank. The street at the moment that my friend left it seemed to go mad with traffic gridlock.

What did the dog have in mind running away like this, when he could have been performing those splendid rushes against the enemy? Indeed, the dog's assaults on traffic, comparable to that of a matador fighting a bull, were perfectly defined public acts of protest against the deteriorating quality of life in the town of Lourdes.

Suddenly I banged the table, scaring nearby patrons. Why, I thought, there could be no doubt about it—my friend How Dare You simply had decided to get away from it all. And why not? Shouldn't he rest too? Don't we all deserve a rest? Why the poor dog did look, come to think of it, weary. He might have been feeling quite upset and possibly a bit discouraged, as all of us get from time to time. Certainly his ears, which were habitually raised and, to me, a sensitive barometer of his moods, were drooping poignantly when he passed me a moment ago. All the combative fire seemed to have gone out of my poor dog.

Never mind—I felt sure that How Dare You was at that moment climbing Pic du Jer, the 3,000 foot mountain situated at the end of town, and there on its summit was resting himself in the silence and solitude of heights, with a fresh Pyrenees breeze to help clear his thoughts....

"Come to me, all you who are weary and
heavy-laden, and I will give you rest...."
This is what you have told us, Lord Jesus.
When life overwhelms us, may we
find our resting place in you.

CHAPTER TWENTY-THREE

Why Did God Choose Lourdes?

August 25. Why did God choose Lourdes from all the rest of the world to dramatize, through Mary, his message of love? Isaiah might have given us a clue when he wrote:

> In days to come the mountain where the Temple stands will be the highest one of all, towering above all the hills. Many nations will come streaming to it, and their people will say, "Let us go up the hill of the Lord, to the Temple of Israel's God. He will teach us what he wants us to do; we will walk in the paths he has chosen." ISAIAH 2:2

Surely Lourdes stands highest among the hills of the Lord's house and, as we know, "many nations come streaming to it" from all over the world. God chose Lourdes so that men and women might gather here, to pray, to worship, to celebrate, to sing his praises. God chose Lourdes as the place to which people of all nations would come in daily procession, seeking his guidance and help through the intercessions of a woman.

One bright sunny morning I climbed the Pic du Jer just

outside the town of Lourdes. I had been told that from there I would have a clear view of the Sanctuary.

I had been told correctly. From Pic du Jer I could see every-thing, not only the Sanctuary with its gleaming steeples but the whole wonderful mountain world of the Pyrenees.

From the mountain top, my eye moved over radically different landscapes: from the plains of the city to gentle hills; from the trimmed, orderly grounds of the Sanctuary to the dark, frozen splendors of the Pyrenees. Here the mountains begin like the spinal column of a gigantic bony beast frozen into the earth—a dark body turning and twisting southward along the borders of France and Spain.

In the center of the Sanctuary stand the double Basilicas with the stillness of a mirage. I could also see the Gave. These river waters, born of many Pyrenees mountain streams, lunge fitfully toward the town of Lourdes. Upon entering the town the waters slow down, widen out in smooth spreading motions, turning themselves around at the foot of the Chateau Fort, whose ram-parts overlook both town and Sanctuary.

As the Gave waters pass round the fort, they take on violence again, springing forth in nervous, violent leaps through the nar-row riverbanks, passing about a hundred feet from the Grotto of the Apparitions, then disappearing into the hills and woodland.

From my vantage point this morning, the land seems to glow with hidden fire. The earth looks freshly hewn. As I gaze, I have the feeling I have seen this land as it was in the beginning: the mountains, the green hills, the valley, the flowering fields. There is a stillness to it, as if this land of the beginning lies under vast layers of time, as if what beauty I see conceals even greater beau-ty, a biding, unsurpassed loveliness that lies invisible, beyond my power to behold. These mountains have the shadow of God's spirit upon them.

The book of Deuteronomy calls the "lasting hills" God's

abode on earth (see Deuteronomy 33:15). In these Pyrenees, hill and mountain stretch out in perfect symmetry, the plains curve and roll in wonderful shapes that never dull the eye. The land sings as though the rocks and faults hide angels in them.

Isaiah writes about such singing: "Let the inhabitants of the rocks sing, let them shout from the top of the mountains" (Is 42:11). The psalmist had this to say: "Great is the Lord, and greatly to be praised in the city of our God, in the mountain of his holiness" (Ps 48:1).

How does Bernadette figure in these lasting hills of God? My thought is that she reflected something of the innocence and beauty of these lasting hills. If you have ever watched children clambering over rocks or running in the fields, you would know that they are in their element, you would see that they move with the step of natural things. They are closer to God's original creation: The birds, the winds, the waters, the mountains—they have not yet left these for the man-made world that we live in, for the artificially invented things that take up our time and dominate our imagination. Whether confined in a room or running free in a meadow, children dwell in a "now" moment and are therefore open to the "small voice" of God. They are, though quite without knowing it, virtually in continual dialogue with this "small voice." Hear them chattering in intimacy with things that we do not see. "Now" moments of children suggest thoughts transparent as air, thoughts which do not weigh, do not cast shadows, thoughts that have not had time to thicken with the cares of this world. Time has not yet wounded them. Without knowing it, children sing choirs with the angels; their laughter tinkles musically like birds musing aloud to one another. Even the silence of a child is transparent and open to the supernatural event, in a way that we adults with our inner disquiets are not.

In her autobiographic accounts, Bernadette describes how the meeting with the Virgin Mary took place. You will see how nature, that is, water, wood, air, mountain, and the Massabielle (called Ancient Rock), the recess from which she saw her Lady, play a significant role in her story. She describes first of all finishing a meal with her family; the fire going out in their miserable hovel; her mother, Madame Soubirous, giving her permission to search for firewood along the Gave. She leaves with her sister Toinette, age 11-1/2, and friend Jeanne Abadie, age 14. They walk as far as the Massabielle and stop where the Savy Canal waters and the little Gave de Pau river converge. Opposite them, on the other side of the waters, stands the Grotto.

Directly in front of the Grotto the girls see piles of the coveted driftwood and fallen branches. Their search is over. But in order for the girls to get the wood they must cross the icy waters of the canal. Bernadette's two companions, after removing stockings and shoes, begin wading across the freezing water in their bare feet. The water is so cold the girls begin to cry.

Bernadette looks for a way to get across without wading in her bare feet. She searches along the banks of the canal for a way across; not finding any, she takes off her shoes. She writes: "Hardly had I taken off my first stocking when I heard a sound as though there had been a rush of wind. I looked round towards the meadow. I saw the stillness of the trees. So I continued to take off my shoes. Again I heard the same noise. I looked up towards the Grotto. I beheld a lady dressed in white. She wore a blue sash and a yellow rose on each foot, matching in color the beads of her rosary. I thought I was mistaken. I rubbed my eyes. But still I saw the same Lady...."[1]

"How fortunate you are!" we hear Jesus say, (Mt 13:11), "Your eyes see and your ears hear. I assure you that many prophets and many of God's people wanted very much to see what you see, but they could not, and to hear what you hear, but they did not." Bernadette saw with her eyes and heard with her ears what many of us want very much to see and hear: We are indebted to her for providing us with an image of the truth of God's love personified in the Virgin Mary. This image of the resurrected Mary attired in her heavenly dress will be with us, thanks to Bernadette, until the end of time.

How wonderful that these visits to Bernadette have made possible good things beyond imagining for so many people. Thanks to these two women, we have with us this jewelled place of opportunity, Lourdes, as one of the few safe harbors for pilgrims to experience every kind of wonderful thing, for revealing many sides of God's love, for making possible many kinds of miracles: relief to the suffering, healing to the sick in body and spirit, light to those in darkness, direction to those confused, truth to seekers, faith to those without it and to those losing it; finally, help for those drawing close to their journey's end, that we might be helped over to the other side of death where, at long last, we shall sit at banquet with Bernadette, and with Bernadette's Lady, and with Jesus at the head of the table, and with all those with whom we traveled our journey, shall partake of the banquet, shall sing with the angels in celebration of God's love forever.

Why did God choose Lourdes? Because every hill and mountain, every valley and stream, every tree and bird, is a prayer of praise to God. Oh, I have no doubt that there are mountains that rise higher, lands that are greener, hills more rolling, cities more ancient in days. These I have not visited. In Lourdes, however, I look upon land lovelier than I have ever seen: Land that lies in fullness and perfection—its rock matured in the centuries, its collossi of mountain, hill, cloud, sky, divinely orchestrated and moving as a single creation. God chose this spot of earth for us because here his handiwork is uniquely beautiful. He chose Bernadette because her soul had kinship with his handiwork, because her innocence could take into herself his light, because her eye could see with God's eye the Virgin Mary. He chose Lourdes so that men and women might gather here, to pray, to worship, to celebrate, to sing God's praises.

On Pic du Jer, this early morning, the voices of the wind go to the four corners of the earth, proclaiming the glory of God. Loosed by God at the beginning of time, the winds come forth out of these Pyrenees—whip out like vast airy boomerangs across the skies. This trembling earth unrolls on a magic carpet of wind. Its booming proclamation resounds with such vigor that the hills take running leaps, skipping over mountains, dancing madly in the skies. The earth and the skies shiver merrily in these winds. The winds have brought all the earth before God, and the earth sings praises to God who made it. The earth's every curve and lineament, every glebe and atom, every vapor and flame, sings. Praise him.

CHAPTER TWENTY-FOUR

Lord, Where Is Your Dwelling Place?

August 27, midnight. I sat in a mood of deep quiet by the Gave, a stone's throw away from the Grotto of the Apparitions, and I glanced up at the shining stars. I was so struck by their beauty and the whole dark wonder of the universe in which they shone, that the words came unbidden to me: "Lord, O Lord, where is your dwelling place?" I scanned the skies, half expecting them to open up with streaming light. The Gospels say clearly that God is in heaven. But where is heaven?

Looking about us in the hard realities of this life, it is difficult to imagine a specific route to heaven. The poets imagine this route beginning somewhere in the skies. The poets might not be far wrong. The kingdom of heaven is a real place, as we read in St. Luke's Gospel. On the night of the birth of Jesus, the shepherds catch a glimpse of the inhabitants of heaven:

> Suddenly a great army of heaven's angels appeared with the angel [speaking to the shepherds], singing praises to God, "Glory to God in the highest heaven, and peace on earth to those with whom he is pleased!" When the angels went

away from them back into heaven, the shepherds said to one another, "Let us go to Bethlehem and see this thing that has happened, that the Lord has told us."   LUKE 2:13-15

This marvelous passage was reported by the shepherds to Joseph and Mary, and later told to Luke. It suggests the existence of a world entirely independent of the physical universe; a world roving freely in the skies and beyond the skies. It is a world rooted not in physical reality as we understand it, but in supernatural reality. "You come from this world," Jesus says, "but I do not come from this world" (Jn 8:23).

Jesus comes to us from another world. The Virgin Mary, described by Bernadette, also comes from this other world. But where is this world? And why do the Gospels take such great pains to tell us, through Jesus, that we must believe in this other world?

Mary's eighteen appearances to Bernadette shed a little light on the mystery of God's dwelling place. The freedom with which she comes and goes, appears and disappears, defies gravity, suspends time, and subjects matter and space to herself reveals a great deal about the other world. All the things that limit us in body and mind, and the things which threaten our spirit with all sorts of dangers, are only temporary. They shall be lifted in heaven; the healings of body and soul that we seek all the days of our life here on earth shall be perfectly completed there. As the book of Revelation tells us:

Behold, the dwelling of God is with men. He will dwell with them, and they shall be his people, and God himself will be with them. He will wipe away every tear from their eyes, and death will be no more, neither shall there be mourning nor crying nor pain any more, for the former things have passed away.   REVELATION 21:3-4

That the people around Bernadette were unable to see the Virgin Mary during her apparitions suggests that they (we) are separated from her by something beyond our imagining. Deep in ourselves we know that we are more than what we appear to one another. All our lives we are tormented by something in us which desires to surpass itself; our physical limitations force us to acknowledge fear, sickness, and death. Being made in the image and likeness of God goads us, and we will not rest until at last we meet him face to face.

The Blessed Mother's freedom is precisely the image and likeness of God's love within herself spiritually realized, spiritually consummated to the highest level of perfection. St. Paul, in 1 Corinthians 2:9, says, "What no man ever saw or heard, what no man ever thought could happen is the very thing God prepared for those who love him."

The Virgin Mary, after Christ, is the first of the fruits of this love. In the Incarnation God took on human flesh; Mary was created as we have been created. Her Son is true man and true God; she is true woman. God raised himself from the dead; Mary was raised by God, as we hope to be raised. The larger issue of her appearances on earth, it seems to me, is to proclaim anew the good news her Son first proclaimed: God is love! She demonstrated this love while she was on earth, and again as a heavenly being. She enters our world in the full power of her resurrected body in order to help us to believe in the existence of the heavenly world from whence she comes.

And where is that world? "I leave the world," Jesus told his followers, "and go to the Father"—which clearly suggested travel. Perhaps not travel in the sense that we understand it, largely because it is spiritual travel. Jesus speaks to this idea in his parable of the mustard seed which suggests movement, change, and growth:

The kingdom of God is like to a grain of mustard seed, which a man took, and sowed in his field, which indeed is the least of all seeds: But when it is grown, it is the greatest among herbs, and becometh a tree, so that the birds of the air come and lodge in the branches thereof.

MATTHEW 13:31

His parable suggests a journey of transformation, invisible and secret, continuing from birth to death and beyond death. God is spinning our eternal body with his truth for the new life. And when our body is ready, it goes to the place Jesus has prepared for it.

Years have passed since that night I sat in the Grotto of the Apparitions and, moved by the beauty of God's world, asked the question, "Lord, O Lord, where is your dwelling place?" The answer is in the promise of Christ that at the appointed time he will come and take us to the other side of death.

"Do not be worried and upset. Believe in God and believe also in me... And after I go and prepare a place for you, I will come back and take you to myself, so that you will be where I am." JOHN 14:1, 3

Come, Lord Jesus, come.

CHAPTER TWENTY-FIVE

In Gratitude to Fellow Pilgrims

September 3. I met and visited with so many wonderful people at Lourdes. All too often we saw each other on the run. Throughout I had a sense that God had brought us together for a special reason, though I did not always discern the reason at the time. I found the sick pilgrims especially transparent in their faith.

Sometimes in wheeling or lifting patients from one place to another, no word passed between us. There wasn't time, or they were too sick to say anything. Yet in a smile or look, they conveyed so much. I saw in them the most profound humility, that is, I saw life in them stripped of all defensive disguises so that I was able to see something of their unique beauty. Although I cannot remember all their names, I shall never forget them.

I remember one Frenchwoman—a big, gray-haired matron— waiting to be placed on the train that would take her home. We had just brought her on the autobus with other patients from the Sanctuary. I stood beside her, waiting for permission to get her safely on board the train. She looked at me so lovingly. Oh, she was so pleased to see an American serving in Lourdes for love of God. Hearing her say "for love of God" made me feel very special indeed!

I asked her what had brought her here. She said that she had cancer in the womb, and put her hands out in a sad gesture of resignation as if to say "that's the way it is." Then she asked me a question: Would I pray for her? Without waiting for me to answer, she motioned for me to come close to her, which I did: Her hands drew me to her, whereupon she planted a kiss on my cheek. Her turn came to be lifted from the platform onto the train. Her hand fluttered good-bye to me as the chair she sat in was pulled backwards through the open door of the train. I have every faith that I will meet this lovely woman some day in the other world.

Then there was Mrs. Downey of Baldwin, New York, a woman about forty-five years old. We were in Rosary Square beside rows of other sick pilgrims waiting for the Procession of the Blessed Sacrament to begin. I overheard her say something and detected her American accent. "You sound like you're from New York," I said. "So do you," she said. In Lourdes making friends has to be done quickly because there's so little time. Perhaps we have just ten minutes to talk and share: We may have to say good-bye and never see each other in this life. And so, I asked the question most often asked in this place: "What are you doing here?"

"What am I doing in Lourdes?" Mrs. Downey smiled. I looked at her. She personified the saying of Jesus found in St. John 17:14, "They do not belong to the world, just as I do not belong to the world." She had a look of one whose traveled spirit had passed through many phases, through many vicissitudes and trials, had long separated herself from all needless attachments to this world. She was therefore free to love, because there was nothing to stop her, because she saw you clear-eyed without fear or distrust. And so in those few minutes I talked and shared with Mrs. Downey, I passed a lifetime with her, so to speak. I felt myself loved by her, and I loved her. It was as if she knew all about me, and I knew all about her. Truly I felt we were in God's presence in the complete well-being of his love.

Why had she come to Lourdes? Almost matter-of-factly, she answered—she had leukemia, and her coming to Lourdes was her last hope. She didn't mind having to die, she explained, it was leaving her husband and children that concerned her. "It will be difficult for them," she said, smiling. And what a smile! This woman through her smile made you see a little of the beauty of God. She had that extraordinary transparency of the self that I have seen in persons who have suffered greatly, a self with nothing to hide, a self that has been purged and purified through its sufferings to a wonderful shining.

I ponder the mystery of suffering, especially when I meet people like Mrs. Downey. In the Gospel of John 9:2-6, there is a fascinating passage which says something about it. "His disciples asked [Jesus], 'Teacher, whose sin was it that caused him to be born blind? His own or his parents' sin?' Jesus answered, 'His blindness has nothing to do with his sins or parents' sins. He is blind so that God's power might be seen at work in him.'"

Immediately following the above passage, Jesus adds these rather cryptic words. "We must keep on doing the works of him who sent me, as long as it is day; the night is coming, when no one can work. While I am in the world I am the light for the world." His words, "The night is coming, when no one can work," are prophetic. Night is a symbol for lack of faith in God's love and power. The world today, a good part of it, lies precisely in this night.

Sometimes my encounters were with people who were not visibly ill, but who carried within them unresolved questions or troubled spirits. I was moved by one young American couple from Minnesota. I met them at Sister Marie's House of Love. One evening I took them to the Candlelight Procession. When we had arrived at the Grotto and were about to begin the public recitation of the Rosary, the young woman turned to me and said, "I wonder if I could ask the Blessed Mother for something."

I could tell that what she wanted to ask was very important. "Ask her for anything," I said. I added, smiling, "I ask her for something every day."

"Well," she whispered to me, "we want a child." I looked into her eyes. I could see the awful pain in them. All I could do was repeat what I had said. "Ask her—ask her for anything." I pray and hope this young couple had their prayers answered.

Then there was Thomas K. from Pennsylvania who had just arrived in Lourdes from visiting the Wailing Wall of Jerusalem.

Thomas was one of two visiting Americans, both young men in their early twenties. I never spoke with his friend, who went ahead of him to London after staying in Lourdes only a few hours. Thomas was easy to talk to, as friendly as a brother. After Lourdes he planned to visit London where he would meet with his friend. And after London, home, Pennsylvania, USA. Then somehow he had to figure out whether he was going to be a priest or not. I asked about his friend. Was his friend thinking of becoming a priest? Thomas' answer was brief: yes.

Thomas in fact stayed in Lourdes a week. "Maybe the Blessed Mother might help me to make up my mind," Thomas said. "You know, it's a big decision." He chatted on. "You know, Americans bypass Lourdes for Rome. Rome has greater traditions, and thousands of years of history. Lourdes is little more than a hundred years old—but I think Lourdes has Rome beat. It has so many kinds of people here from different countries; Lourdes offers the world a kind of United Nations under God."

I never met anyone who anguished more over his vocation. He had a knack for asking questions and leaving them unanswered, such as, "Am I capable of being a priest? Can I be effective? Will it puff me up to be called Father? Can I stick it out all those years until I die? Will I fall in love with a woman and go crazy thinking about her? But, more important, does God want me?" He would conclude this litany of questions with the words, "I have to pray, I have to pray."

Thomas was also tortured by all the suffering he saw around him. "Some of the patients here are so deformed all I can do is stare at them. How can they bear it? And why doesn't God heal them? Why? Why doesn't he? You know, in the Gospels, Jesus heals everybody. Why can't Jesus heal everybody as he did when he walked this earth?"

In another mood he couldn't get over the pilgrims singing and praying and chanting; the praying especially went on day and night. "Here (in Lourdes) one thing is compelling, one thing desired above everything: God. In the United States, we are distracted by everything. We want this, we want that, and everything has a price tag. But not here. Here God is the center of attraction."

He had a wonderful devotion to the Virgin Mary. "The Virgin Mary is great not for seeking her rights but for seeking God's will. She placed loving God and neighbor above everything else. If we could do what she did we would all have life and have it abundantly, exactly as Jesus says. You see, she is greater than we are because she loved more than we do."

He paused, his thoughts taking another turn. "Though we are in Virgin Mary country, and grateful for our faith, it's hard to believe that in other parts of the world, Christ is unknown. I wish I could understand whether salvation comes to all those different peoples who've never heard of Christ. I can't believe they are denied salvation because they happen not to be born in the United States or France or Italy. As a priest—if I ever become a priest—what shall I tell my parishioners if they ask me this?" Long pause. "I guess truth is one, and God is the same for everyone no matter who he is. I shouldn't worry about it."

On his last night in Lourdes we met on the other side of the Gave de Pau to pray and talk. When he saw me the first thing he said was, "Please pray for my vocation." I promised I would. We talked about Vatican II, the role of the lay person, the shortage of priests, the ordination of women, and so on. Then we said the Rosary.

It was time to say good-bye. He suddenly took out of his pocket a carefully folded piece of paper and handed it to me. "The last few times I've come down and watched the water of the river flow. I did yesterday and when I got home I wrote this poem. I call it 'Water of Lourdes.'" He added, "I'm not a poet. I just like to write down my thoughts." He added, "You don't even have to read it if you don't want to." I knew he wanted me to. Here it is:

> *No man can sit by water and not pray.*
> *No man can sit by water and not say with Christ,*
> *"Whoever believes in me will receive living water*
> *and it shall be in you a well of water*
> *springing up into everlasting life."*
> *No Christ without living water.*
> *No river without the city.*
> *No heaven without Christ.*
> *No hope without God.*

There were many other persons I met, both healthy pilgrims and sick pilgrims, and all those thousands of nameless beautiful faces that God let me love through my volunteer work if only for a brief moment. I celebrate them, I am grateful to them, and I give thanks to God for giving me the privilege of serving them.

Notes

TWO
The Algerian Policeman

1. *The Layman's Call to the Apostolate*, 491.
2. *The Layman's Call to the Apostolate*, 491.

SIX
The Spanish Boy Scout

1. *Battle Hymn of the Republic*, Julia Ward Howe (1819-1920).

TEN
A Poor Man Named Francis

1. Alexander Pope, *The First Satire of the Second Book of Horace from The Poetical Works of Alexander Pope*, edited by Adolphus William Ward, (London: MacMillan, 1964), 286.

ELEVEN
The Odd Couple

1. This hymn (of 60 verses), composed by the Abbe Gaignet, professor at the seminary of Lucon (Vendee) was sung for the first time at the Grotto on May 27, 1873. Printed in Guide to Lourdes, Rev. J.A. Shields, 85.

FIFTEEN
All Carry a Cross

1. Henry Suso, *Revelations of the Mystics, The Soul Afire,* edited by H. A. Reinhold (New York: Image, 1973), 152-53.

TWENTY-THREE
Why Did God Choose Lourdes?

1. A. Ravier, S.J., *The Writings of St. Bernadette* (Paris: Lethielleux, 1961), 242.